'Vintage Williams – an antidote for anyone who has ever struggled with Paul himself or with large, complicated books about the apostle! Three beautifully written chapters explain clearly the social world of the man himself, his disturbing idea of the universal welcome in Christ, and his understanding of the new creation brought about through the death and resurrection of Jesus. This simple but profound introduction to Paul will be helpful at any time of year, but the final questions and Bible studies for reflection will greatly assist those wishing to read it during Lent.'

The Revd Canon Professor Richard A. Burridge
Dean of King's College, London

'There are two forms of simplicity. First, there is a certain naive "not knowing" that is yet to encounter the difficulty and challenge of a subject; and then there is another "deeply felt knowing" that sits on the other side of complexity and is only arrived at after much searching and reflection. Here, a subject is known so well that it has become part of the person who tells it. This deceptively simple little book is a wonderful example of this sort of knowing. Rowan Williams seems to have arrived at a point where a lifetime's learning and praying is distilled into profound simplicity.'

The Rt Revd Stephen Cottrell, Bishop of Chelmsford

'In *Meeting God in Paul*, Rowan Williams explains how Paul moved from being the leader of an anti-Christian terrorist squad to being all-consumed by his contemporary, Jesus, who becomes for Paul "the image of the invisible God". This is a most important and much needed book. It releases St Paul from the box of popular misconception and introduces us to Paul as a powerful evangelist who welcomes all who want to follow Christ, and wishes to bar none.'

David Suchet, actor and presenter of the BBC TV series
In the Footsteps of St Paul

'Many people find the complexity of Paul's character a barrier to understanding his writings. Here, Rowan Williams helps us to see that see that Paul's complexity is a gift; that his writings are deep and difficult because we are deep and difficult, and they touch us because they speak to our basic humanity.'

Angela Tilby, Diocesan Canon, Christ Church, Oxford
and regular contributor to BBC Radio 4's 'Thought for the Day'

Born in 1950, Rowan Williams was educated in Swansea (Wales) and Cambridge. He studied for his theology doctorate in Oxford, after which he taught theology in a seminary near Leeds. From 1977 until 1986, he was engaged in academic and parish work in Cambridge, before returning to Oxford as Lady Margaret Professor of Divinity. In 1990 he became a fellow of the British Academy.

In 1992 Professor Williams became Bishop of Monmouth, and in 1999 he was elected as Archbishop of Wales. He became Archbishop of Canterbury in late 2002 with ten years' experience as a diocesan bishop and three as a primate in the Anglican Communion. As archbishop, his main responsibilities were pastoral – whether leading his own diocese of Canterbury and the Church of England, or guiding the Anglican Communion worldwide. At the end of 2012, after ten years as archbishop, he stepped down and moved to a new role as Master of Magdalene College, Cambridge.

Professor Williams is acknowledged internationally as an outstanding theological writer and teacher as well as an accomplished poet and translator. His interests include music, fiction and languages.

Meeting God in Paul

Reflections for the Season of Lent

ROWAN WILLIAMS

WJK WESTMINSTER
JOHN KNOX PRESS
LOUISVILLE • KENTUCKY

First published in the United States of America in 2015 by
Westminster John Knox Press
100 Witherspoon Street
Louisville, KY 40202

First published in Great Britain in 2015 by
Society for Promoting Christian Knowledge
36 Causton Street
London SW1P 4ST

15 16 17 18 19 20 21 22 23 24—10 9 8 7 6 5 4 3 2 1

Unless otherwise noted, Scripture quotations are the author's own translation.

Cover design by designpointinc.com
Typeset by Graphicraft Limited, Hong Kong

Library of Congress Cataloging-in-Publication Data

Names: Williams, Rowan, 1950– author.
Title: Meeting God in Paul : reflections for the season of Lent / Rowan
   Williams.
Description: Louisville, KY : Westminster John Knox Press, 2015. | Includes
   bibliographical references.
Identifiers: LCCN 2015047739 (print) | LCCN 2015048291 (ebook) | ISBN
   9780664260538 (alk. paper) | ISBN 9781611646726 ()
Subjects: LCSH: Bible. Epistles of Paul--Criticism, interpretation, etc. |
   Paul, the Apostle, Saint. | Lent.
Classification: LCC BS2650.52 .W58 2015 (print) | LCC BS2650.52 (ebook) | DDC
   227/.06--dc23
LC record available at http://lccn.loc.gov/2015047739

Most Westminster John Knox Press books are available at special quantity discounts when purchased in bulk by corporations, organizations, and special-interest groups. For more information, please e-mail SpecialSales@wjkbooks.com.

Contents

Introduction

Trying to write a very short book about St Paul feels a bit risky: from the early centuries of the Christian Church until now, the great minds of Christianity have worked out their thoughts in lengthy and impassioned dialogue with Paul's letters, and the quantity and quality of their reflection is a reminder of just how much there is to discover in these unique documents. My dear friend and former colleague, Tom Wright, has recently produced a magisterial study of Paul, practically every one of whose nearly 1,700 eloquent pages contains some fresh and challenging insight requiring more thought and exploration from the reader. Can anything useful be achieved in a few brief chapters?

The only excuse for a brief study like this is that Paul's world remains a closed book for so many regular churchgoers – never mind the numerous others who hear Paul's name and are distantly aware that he was important at the beginnings of Christianity. Both believers and non-believers are quite likely to have picked up a set of assumptions about Paul – that he had a problem about women's role in the Church, that he was against sex in general and homosexuality in particular, that he supported slavery, that he changed the simple teaching of Jesus into a complicated philosophy or mythology, and so on. There are plenty of good twenty-first-century reasons, it seems, to write him off.

But in fact these half-understood assumptions obscure nearly everything of what makes Paul really interesting and exciting. I believe that we need to read Paul with a sense of his own intense conviction that he was exploring a new country – as fertile, beautiful and exhilarating, above all as real and tangible in its working, as any that a sixteenth-century sailor might have run across in his voyages of discovery. Did Paul transform Christianity? Yes, of course. He took a bundle of traditions and practices generated by the mysterious events around and after Jesus' death and struggled, with all the intellectual and imaginative skill he could muster, to see the patterns that held them together. But the more you read him, the more you see how he is labouring to do justice to something that is already there confronting him in these stories and practices – not improvising a new religious system. Sometimes there are still loose ends in his attempts to bring it all together in a consistent pattern; more often he uncovers a set of interconnections so profound that they have set the agenda for centuries of further discussion and elaboration. He is never looking for new religious theories for their own sake; he is always asking what *must* be true about God, about Jesus, about the human and the non-human world, if the prayer and practice of the early Christians he knew is to make some kind of sense, to them as well as to their baffled or suspicious neighbours.

And to grasp how this works, we need to have at least some sense also of the social world and the world of ideas Paul inhabits. He will take for granted things we don't think about; he will, at the same time, challenge things that everyone else in his era took for granted. It helps to have some feeling for this, otherwise we shall miss the moments when he is being most courageous and creative, when the dangerous newness of what has happened because of Jesus most clearly comes through for him.

So what I have attempted to do here is to sketch in a bit of that background, in the hope that the reader will emerge with a better sense of that 'dangerous newness' – of why Christians believed that the events involving Jesus completely changed the framework within which they lived; and then to trace some of the specific ways in which both behaviour and language in the Christian community were being remoulded day by day under the pressure of the way Christians had learned to pray. Paul is exceptionally original in the way he allows this question to shape his thinking – and he reminds the modern Christian that theological language withers and dies when it is not conscious of the pressure upon it of the way we pray. I hope the result will convey a little of the energy and freshness of Paul's witness to Jesus and the God he encountered in Jesus.

A note on Paul's letters

Because there has been so much debate in the last couple of hundred years about whether all of the letters attributed to Paul in the New Testament are really written by him, it may be helpful to set out a few of the basic assumptions I will be making about these letters as we refer to them throughout this book. Everybody agrees that Romans, 1 and 2 Corinthians, Galatians and the brief note to Philemon are from Paul's hand, and most agree that the first and second letters to the church in Thessalonica are authentic. That leaves the three 'prison letters', as they are sometimes called, supposedly written by Paul in jail in Rome – the letters to Ephesus, Colossae and Philippi – Ephesians, Colossians and Philippians; and also the letters to Timothy and Titus, usually called the 'Pastorals'.

I shan't elaborate the details of the scholarly controversies, not least because there seems almost no possibility of complete certainty. But it is really important to remember in this context that our assumptions and those of the first Christian century are not always identical. When we are faced with the claim that one of Paul's letters is not really by Paul, we in the twenty-first century tend to think, 'So it's a forgery.' That is not exactly how people would have thought at the time. Somebody who saw himself as a loyal disciple of Paul might very well put together what he believed to be an authentic and truthful digest of what the great apostle taught, and say, 'This is Paul.' Or somebody might string together fragments of letters that Paul had written, add some connecting passages and say, 'This is Paul.' That's the way in which many people's minds worked at the time, so that to say that a text is not entirely composed of words written by Paul is definitely not to say that it is a forgery in anything like the modern sense. And we do have some examples from the early Christian world of texts that were acknowledged to be forgeries – written to deceive or mislead or simply to propagandize for specific views. The early Christians had some ways of telling the difference between a text that had something credible about it that related it to the real world of the supposed author and another that just used the name to advance a set of views.

For what it's worth, my own conclusion is that most of the literature under Paul's name actually does originate with him. Unfashionably, I believe that the letter to Ephesus is from Paul, though written by Paul in collaboration with someone else polishing his style and clarifying and extending his ideas. The other two 'prison letters' I think deserve the benefit of the doubt, though some uncertainty remains. The letters to Timothy and Titus are in some ways the hardest to deal with. They seem to be examples of what I just mentioned – fragmentary notes from Paul written up with connecting passages; but they also seem to introduce ideas that Paul might have found unfamiliar, and their vocabulary is often a long way from the way Paul writes in the letters we can be sure of. There are enough vivid personal touches in those letters to make you reluctant to write them off completely, but there are phrases there which are so unlike the Paul of Romans or Galatians, even when every allowance has been made for an older man writing, that it is quite hard to believe that the same pen wrote them. Yet that doesn't mean that they are not 'apostolic' documents or, if you are a Christian, *inspired* documents, part of an inspired Scripture. It simply means that the process by which we have got them is a bit more complicated than just Paul writing things down and somebody else copying them on.

In this little book I will be depending quite heavily on the major letters that are undoubtedly Paul's as they stand – Romans, the Corinthian letters, Galatians – but without ignoring the three prison letters and the little personal note to Philemon. I don't believe the theology of the letters to Timothy and Titus is completely incompatible with what is in these texts; but it is at least very differently expressed and carries a number of different assumptions, so I shall be referring less often to these.

Biblical quotations are versions of my own.

Once again, Philip Law and the staff of SPCK have generously encouraged and assisted the process of putting a brief series of Canterbury Cathedral lectures into publishable shape; and Jonathan and Sarah Goodall have helped immensely in transcribing and tidying up these talks. In understanding Paul, I owe a great debt to my first New Testament teachers, especially the late Charlie Moule and John Sweet; and to all with whom I have discussed Paul's thought over the years, particularly Tom Wright, Tony Thiselton and Kathy Grieb, whose books as well as conversation continue to enrich my reading so deeply. As with earlier books of mine emerging from Holy Week in Canterbury, I want to express thanks to the cathedral family and to all who attended the lectures, asked questions and offered new insights.

Rowan Williams
Cambridge
Eastertide 2015

1

Outsiders and insiders: Paul's social world

Whenday light came, the magistrates sent their officers with the order 'Release those men.' The jailer reported these instructions to Paul: 'The magistrates have sent an order for your release. Now you are free to go in peace.' But Paul said to the officers: 'We are Roman citizens! They gave us a public flogging and threw us into prison without trial. Are they now going to smuggle us out by stealth? No indeed! Let them come in person and escort us out.' The officers reported his words to the magistrates. Alarmed to hear that they were Roman citizens, they came and apologized.   (Acts 16.35–39)

Paul the Roman citizen

Paul was very proud of his status as a Roman citizen, and if we are going to understand something about the world he lived in, and the assumptions with which people worked in that world, we need to understand a little about Rome and Roman citizenship. It is so important to Paul that we find him mentioning it in three places in the stories in the Acts of the Apostles. I have just quoted Acts 16.35 ff., the story

3

of Paul's adventures in Philippi, where he was arrested and imprisoned; here he is protesting indignantly at his treatment. And if you look at Acts 21.39 and Acts 22.25 you will find the same story – Paul being manhandled and mistreated by Roman soldiers or Roman officials, and stopping them short by saying, 'Before you push me around any further, you'd better be aware that I am a Roman citizen.'

These are stories which remind us that the great thing about being a Roman citizen was that you had certain kinds of guaranteed protection – privileges and liberties that were not available to everybody. You were clearly different from slaves; but you were also different, for example, from that rather loose class of people that the Romans called *peregrini* (the origin of our word 'pilgrims') – a word that essentially just means 'outsiders'. These would be people who lived in the towns and cities but didn't have the rights of citizens; they might be migrant workers, or foreigners of some other kind.

So even within the Empire there were lots of different ways of belonging (or half-belonging) – slaves, migrants, citizens. And by the time you got to the barbarians who lived outside the Roman borders (frightful people like Celts), then of course you were in an entirely different world. But what sort of liberties and protections did citizens enjoy? If you were a citizen, for example, you could make a will – you could do what you liked with your property and leave it to whom you wanted. You could sue people in the law courts – usually a rather expensive business because you had to pay out considerable sums of money in bribes and sweeteners for the magistrates (unfortunately, you could also *be* sued in the law courts, which was at least as expensive for exactly the same reasons). You could marry without asking anybody's permission. You could vote. You could stand for election. You could travel, and if you went to another city within the Roman Empire which was regarded as being of equal status to the one you had just left, you could exercise all your rights as a citizen there as well. Being a Roman citizen was a bit like having a British passport in the early twentieth century – you could go more or less anywhere and expect to be treated properly. Being a citizen was no small matter. And if we are to understand Paul's world, we have to understand first and foremost that this is a world in which *nothing* exists that corresponds to our idea of universal human rights. There was no such thing as general equality before the law. Being a citizen guaranteed you many things; being a *peregrinus*, a migrant or a low-paid worker gave you a few limited privileges before the law; and being a slave gave you none at all.

There were various ways of acquiring citizenship, and once again we hear a bit about it in the Acts of the Apostles (Acts 22.28), where a Roman army officer says to Paul that it cost him a great deal of money to buy his rights as a citizen and Paul replies, with what sounds like some disdain, that he was *born* a citizen. If that little detail is an accurate report (and there is no particular reason to think otherwise), it suggests that his family had probably been settled in Tarsus for quite a long time; because it was in 66 BC that all the inhabitants of Tarsus, in what is now south-eastern Turkey, were given citizenship rights by the Roman government.

Paul probably came from a family that was reasonably well to do but not so rich that he didn't have to earn his living. His family is clearly well off enough to send him to Jerusalem for a long period of training in traditional Jewish scholarship, but we also learn that he had acquired a trade as a tent maker (Acts 18.3). So he is moderately comfortable, on the edges of the upper artisan class, some spare money going around, but above all – the crucial distinction – a citizen. Set that alongside the other two classes. If you were a migrant, a *peregrinus*, you could move around but you had no guarantee that your legal status would remain the same. You couldn't vote, you couldn't make a will – when you died your property would be confiscated by the city. You could be tortured, which a Roman citizen couldn't be. And you could be subject to any number of painful and humiliating forms of execution, including crucifixion, which was not a punishment given to citizens. Hence Paul is able to travel freely and to work with the expectation of some security; and when he is arbitrarily arrested or punished, he can claim that his civic rights have been infringed.

Citizenship was not a matter of class or income in our sense. There would be citizens who were not very well off, and there would be migrants and even some slaves who were quite well off. It was a matter of security and identity: a matter of what you could take for granted without worrying. It was a distinction most visible in urban life, in the life of the cities – and we need to remember that the cities of Paul's time were very mixed, very cosmopolitan. We mustn't fall into the trap of thinking that the world of the New Testament was a world of simple Oriental peasants and ancient Romans in togas. It was a world commercially very active, culturally very creative, where languages and traditions mingled freely within the life of the cities, held together rather unstably by two main things: the authority of the Roman Emperor and the Greek language.

It was a rather odd kind of Greek by the standards of classical Greece, but nonetheless an effective medium for communication. I suppose you could compare its development with the way in which the English language has gone through a number of startling and surprising transformations as a language of commerce and trade, let's say, in South East Asia. Anyone who has ever spent any time in Singapore will recognize that there are very vigorous forms of English spoken there which are not exactly those of the Home Counties. The Greek that St Paul and his associates spoke would have been that kind of language: vigorous, crisp and often eloquent – but not quite classical.

As we have seen, divisions within this world weren't a matter of wealth and income. Some non-citizens had quite a lot of money from trade, but they couldn't dispose of it simply as they wanted. They could be mobile – they could take their business around the Empire, like St Paul's friends Aquila and Priscilla, whom we meet in several places in the New Testament (first of all in Acts 18, and they turn up again in Romans 16; most readers find them an irresistibly appealing couple, sensible, hospitable and entirely supportive of Paul, Apollos and others). But we don't know whether they were citizens; probably they weren't – because they had been exiled from Rome along with other Jews by the Emperor Claudius. So they move around the Empire as traders, and they clearly have quite a lot of disposable income. They have a house big enough for the community to meet in (Romans 16.5), and they can obviously give generous support to wandering apostles. Nonetheless, if they lacked citizenship, they would have been far more insecure than the wandering teacher Paul.

Worst of all, of course, was the position of the slave. The slave, we should never forget, is literally the *property* of someone else. The slave has no rights of movement or travel. The slave can only travel with the master's licence. A slave cannot marry, except with the master's consent. A slave, if brought up before the law courts, is routinely tortured – and I do mean routinely: it was assumed that no slave would tell the truth unless forced to do so (they would after all be legally bound to defend their masters or mistresses), so if they were giving legal evidence, the default position was that they would have to be tortured. In extreme circumstances they could be killed with impunity by their owners. In cultivated Roman circles, it was regarded as rather bad form – as well as economically foolish – to put the lives of your slaves at risk or kill them, but the sanctions were social rather than moral or legal. And of course the body of the slave, male or female, was entirely at the disposal of the master, or indeed mistress, for sexual services.

A slave might well be highly educated. A master might decide to invest in a slave, to expose him to all the best resources of classical education so that he could be a tutor to the younger generation or a resourceful and professional business manager, or so that he could help a master write his memoirs. A slave could in some circumstances accumulate money, and therefore could sometimes buy his or her freedom. But that depended on whether the master would allow it or not. If the master was in trouble with the law, the slave was liable to share his punishment. If a master was convicted of treason in the Roman Empire, it was not unknown for the whole household to be executed – in the case of slaves, probably by crucifixion.

That was the world of the Roman Empire and its great cities, the world Paul inhabits – a world which is more strange to us and our assumptions than we might ever have guessed from the pages of the Bible alone. And these points about the legal status of different groups in the Empire are worth labouring if only to underline the point I made earlier: this is a world that has no conception of universal human rights or dignities – a world in which where you fitted into the social pattern determined pretty well everything about you.

I shan't at this stage say very much about what Paul does with all this in his teaching, but there is one thing that is worth noting before I pass on. The evidence of a letter like Paul's first letter to the Christians in Corinth makes it very clear that urban Christian communities included people of very diverse social background and status. Paul, with the inimitable tactlessness he can sometimes show, reminds the Corinthians in the first chapter of his first letter to them (1.26) that not many of them came from respectable or well-born backgrounds. Later on in chapter 6 he rattles off a list of disreputable styles of behaviour and says, 'Such were some of you.' The impression is that the community in Corinth had quite a strong representation of non-citizen groups: shop-keepers, migrant workers, household slaves. But also in 1 Corinthians 6 we find St Paul being strongly critical of Christians who choose to go to law to settle disputes – which must mean that it included *citizens* who had the right to institute legal proceedings. So, if you begin with the picture of Roman society I have been sketching, and turn to something like the first letter to Corinth, you will see how eccentric the Christian community would have looked to almost anybody in the world around at the time. A place in which slaves and citizens, traders and migrant workers, mingled together; a very rare place indeed (but more of that in the next chapter).

Paul the Jew

Paul is a Roman citizen – but he also, of course, inherited another very stratified and very strict tradition. He is a Jew: a Jew whose name was originally Saul, and who, he tells us, came initially from the tribe of Benjamin (Philippians 3.5). He belongs to that huge class of Jewish entrepreneurs and traders, merchants, travellers and teachers called 'the Diaspora' – the Jewish people dispersed around the Mediterranean in the centuries just before the beginning of the Christian era. As I have said, the likelihood is that his family had been settled in Tarsus for some time. Tarsus was an obvious place for traders and others to settle. Tucked into the corner of south-east Turkey, it was a great regional centre, a major trading city. It had been given privileges by the Roman government in the century before Christ; and it is in fact the place where Antony first met Cleopatra. So when Paul, speaking to the Roman commander, says that he is a citizen of (in the old translation) 'no mean city', we see what was in his mind. Tarsus had amphitheatres and baths and paved streets, a reputation and a resident governor.

But Paul seems to have spent quite a bit of his early adulthood in Jerusalem. He refers to having 'sat at the feet of Gamaliel' (Acts 22.3), and we know Gamaliel from earlier in the Acts of the Apostles (Acts 5.34–39) as a member of the Jewish Council who advises against punishing the early Christians severely, famously advising, 'Let's see how this turns out, because if it comes from God, it is going to work and we are going to look very foolish.' But we also hear about Gamaliel from Jewish sources: we know that he was the grandson of the great Hillel, perhaps the most famous of the first-century Jewish rabbis, and that he inherited a lineage of teaching and tradition which took a fairly gentle and moderate view of the legal obligations binding on religious Jews. There are several stories in Jewish texts about the rivalry between Hillel's disciples and those of Shammai, a much more rigorous teacher. Gamaliel emerges in the Jewish texts as a very impressive figure indeed. There is one text that says, 'Since the death of Rabbi Gamaliel, true knowledge of the law has passed away from Israel.' And yet, oddly, we have very few specific judgements ascribed to Gamaliel, as if his reputation was just a little bit clouded – and it is tempting to think that this had something to do with the fact that he had recommended clemency towards the early Christians, perhaps even that he had been the teacher of the notorious 'Saul from Tarsus'.

But if Paul had been a student at the feet of this gentle and irenic character, how on earth did he become such a savage enemy of the early Church, the community which his master and teacher had been so understanding about? Paul's own admission is that he was a violent persecutor (1 Corinthians 15.9). This, though, is where we have to read the Acts of the Apostles very carefully; and, if we do that, there is a fair bit of evidence that at this particular moment in the history of the early Church some unusual alliances were being formed. Remember the great speech that Stephen gives to the Jewish Council in chapter 7 of the Acts of the Apostles after he has been arrested for his preaching – a speech in which this enthusiastic and rather reckless Christian teacher explains why the coming of Jesus has made the worship of the Jerusalem Temple a thing of the past, and also argues that the death and resurrection of Jesus display the religious experts as being, in effect, traitors to their own tradition. It is very strong stuff indeed; it was certainly calculated to annoy the priests who ran the Temple – but it was also calculated to annoy those who laid great emphasis on keeping the law in full rigour. In other words, Stephen alienated both the Sadducees (the priestly class) and the Pharisees (the lay enthusiasts), and it seems as if, at that point, there is a tactical alliance between the priests and at least some of the powerful leaders among the lay experts. In this situation, the young Saul becomes something of a 'bridge' figure: 'a young man named Saul', as he is described when we first meet him. As Stephen is stoned to death and the witnesses who begin the stoning strip off their clothes, they lay them at the feet of a young man named Saul (Acts 7.58).

This young man is the one who is to pursue the policies of the chief priests against the Christian Church, and we read in Acts 9 of the ferocity with which this was done. It's not difficult to imagine the very deep tensions in the mind of this young man. Brought up as a rather liberal Pharisee, he is now allying himself with the corrupt hierarchy of the Temple which the Pharisees normally disapproved of heartily – and that must have been a hard place to be. It is significant that when, later on, he himself appears before the Jewish Council in Acts chapter 23, he quite deliberately provokes a quarrel between the two parties in the Council, setting the Pharisees and Sadducees against each other; he knows from the inside just how deep those divisions run and where the faultlines are.

So I don't think that Paul's record as a persecutor of the Church suggests that the story of his relationship with Gamaliel is untrue. On the contrary, it's not at all unusual for a gifted and enthusiastic student to revolt very sharply against a revered teacher. And there, in the story of Stephen's speech, we have what may have been the watershed, the provocative moment, when Paul realized that he could not go along with his old teacher's tolerant attitude to this new heretical group; the moment when he decided he would, against all his instincts, have to throw in his lot with what his colleagues regarded as the wealthy, greedy and self-perpetuating priestly caste of the Temple.

I've alternated in the last few pages between the two names, Saul and Paul. It wasn't at all unusual for a Jew living in the Diaspora to have a name used in the family and in the synagogue – a Jewish name – and a name for public consumption – an official Roman name. 'Paulos' is a common enough Roman name (and indeed in chapter 13 of the Acts of the Apostles Paul meets a Roman governor with that very name), but 'Sha'ul' (Saul, the name of the first king of Israel) would be the name used in his family and no doubt in Gamaliel's classroom. It is a practice that survived in many Jewish families in Europe well into the twentieth century and is still common in some Jewish contexts.[1]

So Paul has a ready-made second identity. He is Paulos, a citizen, a traveller, an artisan, as well as being Sha'ul, a Jewish teacher, an expert in the law – and for a brief, hectic and heady period, the leader of what is almost a terrorist snatch squad. But the point is that the Jewish world Paul inhabits is just as strictly defined and layered as the Roman world. It is a world where social identities matter immensely, marked by fierce quarrels about who is a real insider, who is a real Jew, who has the real authority to settle disputes – priests, lawyers, sages? Paul belongs in a world where it is of first importance to know exactly where you stand. Inside or outside? A citizen or a migrant? A free person or a slave? A Jew or a Gentile? A Pharisee or a Sadducee? A man or a woman? A world where the lines are deeply etched and there is very little possibility of crossing them, a world of complex identity politics.

I suggested that we might turn to the first letter to Corinth to see some of the light that is thrown on the text by the social background in the cities of the Empire; and in relation to Paul's Judaism, we might turn to the longest (and most difficult) of his letters, that to the Romans. It is here, in his letter to the Romans, that Paul presses hardest and most steadily on the nerve, the question that must have made him personally most uncomfortable: what is it that makes Jews distinctive or superior? He is driven increasingly to challenge the inside–outside disjunction in which he has been educated, asking, 'Do you think that because you are a law-keeping rigorist within the Jewish world this gives you some purchase on God and the favour of God? Think again.' But at the same time: 'Do you think that because you're a Gentile welcomed into the Christian community by God's free grace this gives you some kind of advantage over the Jew? Think again.'

You can read the whole of the letter to the Romans and hear it as Paul turning his head from side to side, saying to Jew and Gentile alike, 'You think you have grounds for feeling superior; let me tell you you're not. Just because I'm telling them that *they* are not superior don't go thinking *you* are.' And so he goes on, chapter after chapter, swivelling his artillery from side to side. It is one of the things that make the letter to the Romans very hard – but also very exhilarating and challenging – reading.

These are some of the main aspects of Paul's social world, Roman and Jewish; and I think you may see why I have entitled this first chapter 'Insiders and outsiders', because such categories mattered intensely to Paul's contemporaries. They were literally matters of life and death, determining where your security lay, the rights you could claim, the advantages you believed you had.

Paul the man

But what of Paul himself? What kind of a person was he? So far we've been sketching out the whole environment, leaving in the middle of it all a human-sized shadow. What kind of man? What age? What do we know of his personal life? St Luke in the Acts calls him 'a *young* man named Saul'. If Stephen was killed in Jerusalem around the year AD 34, as seems likely, not very long after Jesus' crucifixion, then Paul was a 'young' man at this date. In the ancient world you definitively stopped being 'young' at the age of 40; so we can conclude that in AD 34 Saul of Tarsus was at most in his 30s. It is a reasonable guess that he was about the same age as Jesus would have been, perhaps a little younger. Jesus, born in probably 7 or 6 before the Christian era, would have been between 33 and 40 at the time of his crucifixion. If Paul was a little younger, born after 6 BC, he is perhaps in his mid 30s when we first meet him.

And his personal life? We know from the first letter to Corinth that he did not have a wife, that he had chosen not to have a wife to take with him on his travels, contrasting his situation with that of St Peter and others (1 Corinthians

7.8, 9.5). Given his rabbinic upbringing, the most likely theory is that he was a widower, and nothing in the first letter to Corinth tells against that – when he writes to single people he explicitly includes both those who have never been married and widowers. I think there is a reasonable case for thinking that that was his own situation.

We know that his health was uncertain. We know that when he arrived in Galatia, so he tells us in his letter to Christians in the region (Galatians 4.13–14), he was suffering from an ailment which was something of a challenge to his hearers. What was this? It could have been epilepsy, as some have suggested; it could also have been some kind of eye disease which would distort his face. Interestingly, there are a couple of cases in the Acts of the Apostles where Paul is described as 'looking intently', or 'peering' or 'screwing up his eyes' (for example Acts 23.1); and it may be no accident that he describes the Galatians as having been ready to tear out their eyes and give them to him (Galatians 4.15). It is not at all unlikely that he suffered from one of the countless forms of eye disease carried by parasites in the Middle East, which again would explain why he looked rather unattractive with swollen eyes and perhaps pus-laden eyelids. Famously, in his second letter to Corinth, he writes (12.7 ff.) of having been given a 'thorn in the flesh' – a long-standing ailment which was humiliating and restricting for him. Whether it was epilepsy, eye disease, lameness or some other kind of disability we don't know. We do know, though, that his health was a matter of concern and seems regularly to have got in the way of his work.

We don't know what he looked like; but there is an intriguing text from quite early in the second century, originating in Asia Minor, which preserves a description of Paul as he approaches the city, about to meet the formidable Thekla, one of his early female converts according to this post-biblical tradition.[2] We are told that he is a little man, bow-legged, thin-faced, hook-nosed, bald with heavy eyebrows meeting in the middle; and this is how he is invariably depicted in the most ancient Byzantine artistic tradition and in icons of him up to the present day. Whether there is any historical background to it we can have no idea, but it has felt plausible to generations.

And as a personality? A passionate man, powerfully, even overwhelmingly impressive in some ways, despite his admitted weakness as a public speaker (2 Corinthians 10.10, 11.6); and sometimes, on the basis of the letters, manipulative and possessive. When his anger runs away with him he can be seriously abusive towards his enemies (Galatians 5.12 is one of the more dramatic examples); even when his anger isn't quite running away from him, he can be fairly fierce. Beginning a chapter in his letter to the Galatians (3.1) with the words 'You idiots' is perhaps not the best way of getting the sympathy of his readers. But that forcefulness, that passion, is also shown in the way in which he expresses his fury at the way in which people he loves are being manipulated or mistreated by others. And whenever you are tempted to lose patience with Paul, turn to some of those passages, especially in 2 Corinthians such as 11.20–21, where he lists the abusive activities of some of his rivals and says, in effect, with massive sarcasm, 'Would you like *me* to treat you like that? I'm sorry: I'm not strong enough.' Just a little before this (11.11), he speaks of the efforts and sacrifices he has made for his flock, and ends, 'Do you think I do this because I don't love you? God knows I do!' And it is this sense of warmth, of generous indignation on behalf of others, that is finally one of the most compelling features of Paul's personality – as, again in 2 Corinthians (11.29), he writes, 'Is there anybody who is made to stumble in their faith, and I do not burn with indignation?' You sense the profound instinctive generosity of the man underlying all the passion and the anger and the occasional manipulative or savage moments.

It is always worth remembering that Paul didn't know he was writing the Bible; that's to say that, when he is writing (or rather dictating) his letters, what we have is a flow of argument which, because Paul is an emotional man, sometimes gets so tangled in its expression that a sentence breaks off and you have to start all over again. It can be hard to follow his grammar, and there are some places where sentences are not quite complete. Again, there can be a point, as in the argument in 1 Corinthians about women covering their heads in public meetings (11.16), where Paul seems to realize that he has got himself into far too complicated a place to explain fully, so breaks off and says, 'If anyone wants to argue further about this, all I have to say is that I don't know anyone who does it' – and moves on hastily.

He doesn't know he is writing the Bible: which – to pick up an earlier point – doesn't mean that this is not inspired Scripture; it simply means that Paul is not taking care over the details of his composition. There are passages of enormous elegance and eloquence: the great hymn about love in 1 Corinthians 13, known to every reader of the New Testament; passages where you can see he is working on how he says things and making it very beautiful; but also passages where he is so absorbed in his wrestling with the nature and purposes and presence of God that the grammar and some of the logical footwork disappears over the horizon.

But that is part of the humanity of Paul – of which I hope, in this first chapter, I have given you some flavour. He is unmistakably, in his letters, a three-dimensional figure, one of the people in the ancient world we know most about, and certainly one of the very few apart from emperors and great public men that we can apprehend with this degree of personal vividness. He is not, therefore, as they say, a plaster saint. He is a man of deep emotions; and, like all people of deep emotions, clearly finds it quite complicated to operate in a very rigid and restrictive social world. But a man who, out of all that passion and that sense of living among anguished contradictions, will bring to birth in his thinking and writing a world which is indeed, as his opponents protest in the Acts of the Apostles (17.6), a world turned upside down.

Religion: none

There is one last aspect of Paul's world which we need to register before moving on, and it is one of the more difficult to grasp for a contemporary reader of the Bible. We have thought about how Paul is presented to us as a Roman citizen, as a Jew and as a human being; but the further odd – and, for our purposes, very important – point to note about Paul's world is that in this context nobody belongs to a 'religion'. There is no such thing as '*a* religion' in the first Christian century. People do religious things; but if you had gone up to somebody in the backstreets of Corinth or Ephesus and asked them the 'census' question, 'What religion are you?' they would have looked at you with complete bafflement. Nobody has 'a religion'. There are, as Paul says wryly in 1 Corinthians 8, countless deities – 'many gods and many lords' – and in his speech in Athens in Acts 17 he says again, very ironically, 'I see that you are very religious in Athens.' But the word that he uses suggests that we translate the phrase as meaning something more like, 'You are very meticulous about keeping in with the gods.'

Because gods are part of the universe; and just as you have to be polite to people who have superior social status (because otherwise they will make your life very difficult), so you'd better be polite to the gods (because they can make your life still more difficult). You may have a favourite among the gods, you may find that the temple of Jupiter is more attractive than the temple of Venus; you may like to go to the festivals there rather more than you like to go to some other temples. Or you might find that it is exciting to sign up as a member of an exotic eastern cult; you might fancy the rites of Mithras and have yourself drenched in the blood of a freshly slaughtered bull. You might, if you were very reckless, decide that you were attracted by the cult of the goddess Cybele, perhaps to be slightly deterred when you found out that the price of being a cleric in this particular group was that you had to be a eunuch. But none of these things had anything much to do with what we now think of as *belonging* to a religion: these groups were not, in the drab language of modern government, 'faith communities'. Being religious was part of being a citizen – or a slave, or whatever: part of being a person in the Roman world. You have to sort out your relationships with and your obligations to the gods, just as you have to sort out these things with anything and everyone. But there is little system to it; except in unofficial cults, there is nothing you could call 'membership', no special social territory where you occupy yourself in 'being religious' as a distinct activity, a kind of leisure activity. For the overwhelming majority of people, there is nothing corresponding to regularly 'going to church' (or mosque or synagogue). There was one exception, of course:

if you were Jewish, you *did* go to the synagogue each week as a matter of practice but that would be part of *being Jewish*, part of the community life into which you were born, not signing up to a religion. The fact that in the Roman world people sometimes converted to Judaism was distinctly odd for Romans. What could it mean to ask for entry into another ethnic group? This was probably the nearest thing you could find in that world to what we now understand by adopting a religion, but it was a serious eccentricity in the eyes of most. The language of conversion from one religion or world-view to another was simply not available in the sense we give it today. Probably the nearest we would get to this would be the religious world, say, of India, with its huge profusion of gods and goddesses, its little informal groups of devotees attached to this or that practice or tradition, and its stubborn and total refusal to think of religion as something segregated from everything else. You belong in your society; and part of the belonging is that you do religious things just as you do other sorts of things.

So what Paul preached was not a new 'religion'. As we shall see, it was a new world order, a new way of belonging with God and one another. It took time to work out exactly what this meant in relation to the god-directed practices of the world around, the 'many gods and many lords' whose shrines could be found in every street and whose festivities punctuated the calendar. We see Paul in 1 Corinthians picking his way carefully through some of these questions: the Roman gods are either empty fictions or devils to him – on either account, we shouldn't give them too much attention. But in a world where religious actions were everywhere present, this created major and minor embarrassments in social life that had to be clarified with the minimum of offence or pointless risk. Paul has to make it crystal clear that the traditional religious practices are simply not possible for anyone who has committed himself or herself to Christ. But this is not because he has invented a new religion that is unhelpfully 'exclusive'; it is because he believes that he and other believers have simply entered a new reality in which quite a lot of what everyone took for granted about their social world was about to be dissolved and reconstructed. So we shall look next at just what it was about Paul's teaching that had so drastic an effect.

2

*The universal welcome:
Paul's disturbing idea*

There is no such thing as Jew and Greek, slave and free man, male and female. For you are all one in Christ Jesus.   (Galatians 3.28)

Breaking down the barriers

The words just quoted form one of the most familiar texts from St Paul's letters – a text which, as you can immediately see, sets Paul in opposition to some of the most powerful and dominant trends of his day. This verse pushes back against all the assumptions we were discussing in the previous chapter, the assumptions of a society in which your position was rigidly determined by who you were as Jew or Gentile, citizen or slave, man or woman. Here is Paul saying that there is something you can belong to in which all these different kinds of status are completely immaterial. There is a site where you all meet on one level. And of course, in a slightly different way and a slightly different idiom, this is very much what the preaching of Jesus himself had stressed: Jesus refuses to accept that in order to belong to the people of God you have to start with a bundle of qualifications, ethnic or legal or social. Jesus extends the dignity of fully belonging to the people of God to all kinds of people in whose company the respectable and the pious emphatically did not want to be.

So when people talk – as many will still do – about the great divide between Jesus and Paul, bear in mind that Jesus' opening of the doors to those who were in the eyes of most people 'not qualified' to belong in the people of God lies behind Paul's disturbing idea of a universal welcome. I underline the word 'welcome', because the principle, the energy behind this vision of a new kind of belonging, comes from God's initiative rather than ours. It is God who has provided the means of entry into this community. It is God's welcome, God's initiative, nothing else; not a bland bit of social philosophy, an ideal of 'social inclusion' and no more.

This language of welcoming, of receiving or accepting, is something which Paul clearly likes to use. It comes out very strongly, for example, in the later chapters of the letter to the Romans. Here is Paul in Romans 14, talking about disputes over whether you can eat meat that has been offered in sacrifice in the temples: 'Those who eat meat must not look down on those who do not. And those who do not eat meat must not pass judgement on those who do. For God has accepted them. God has welcomed them' (Romans 14.3).

The one thing you know for certain about your tiresome, annoying, disobedient, disedifying fellow Christians is that

God has welcomed them; that becomes your challenge. Paul spells it out very directly towards the end of his letter to the Romans: 'Accept one another as Christ accepted us to the glory of God' (Romans 15.7). 'Welcome', 'acceptance', 'receiving': the words blend into each other but the central theme is clear: God has received us into the community that he wills and designs; and so our attitude to one another must be consistent with God's, an attitude of welcome or acceptance. And if we recall what was said in our first chapter about insiders and outsiders in the world that Paul inhabited, it is possible to see how this begins to unsettle so many of the dominant ideas of Paul's environment.

If you turn to what are usually called the 'prison letters' of Paul – Ephesians and Philippians and Colossians (the ones whose authorship as they stand is a little less secure) – you'll find, for example in the second chapter of Ephesians, some very strong statements about the bringing down of walls of separation: another way of approaching the same theme. What has happened in the events of Jesus' death and rising is that partitions have been destroyed; people who were far off have turned up next door. The peacemaking which happens through the event of Jesus Christ is the way in which God's welcome, God's initiative, becomes real and active in the world. And we might turn, for a brief moment, to another bit of the New Testament, to the first letter ascribed to St Peter – a text which may itself be influenced by Paul's letter to the Ephesians – to see there in plain words the

31

statement that 'those who were once not a people have now become a people' (1 Peter 2.10). Those who were once strays, migrants, exiles, foreigners, are now insiders. They now belong. They are neither a collection of random individuals nor a group of barely tolerated marginal oddities; they are citizens of a proper civic community. In other words, belonging to God's people is being neither a Jew nor a Gentile; it's a third reality beyond the rival identities of different sorts of insider – the insideness of the Jew confident in God's choice of Israel, the insideness of the Roman citizen. There is something potentially larger than both these kinds of belonging, a new belonging simply as a human being invited by God into intimacy with the eternal. And so this community of God's people is a place where the barriers we take for granted, between insiders and outsiders, superiors and inferiors, break down. The point is made dramatically in a throwaway remark in the tenth chapter of 1 Corinthians (verse 32), where Paul says that he tries to give no offence (and other people shouldn't give offence) to Jews or Greeks *or to the assembly of God*. The human race, it seems, consists of Jews and non-Jews, but now also of those people who are, so to speak, neither Jews nor non-Jews. They are God's assembly: literally, the people who are summoned and invited by God, the people called out by God.

So this is where Paul's thinking about the Christian community begins: it is 'a home for the homeless', to borrow a phrase used as the title for a book on the New Testament church many years ago; a place where the polarities of inside and outside are overcome; and where the one thing you know for certain about your Christian neighbour is that God, incomprehensibly, wants him or her there.

A different kind of freedom

For Paul, then, our basic attitude to our fellow Christians can be summed up in a single word: 'welcome'. But there's another crucial word in Paul's thinking, and that is 'freedom'. The new community, neither Jewish nor Gentile, the new way of belonging together in the company of God, is a community in which people are *delivered from slavery*. Remember, this is not just a metaphor in Paul's time. The idea that by belonging to the community of God you move from being a slave to being a free person presents the most radical change you could imagine in the ancient world. So, in the light of that social background, by saying that we are set free Paul doesn't mean: 'Once I had lots of restrictions and now I can do what I like.' It's much more than that, more like: 'Once I had no power to shape my own life at all. And now I have.'

When Paul writes to the church in Galatia, freedom is at the very centre of his argument in the letter. He is worried that his brothers and sisters there seem to want to be slaves again, and he demands, angrily and passionately, 'What is going on?' No wonder that he addresses the Galatians as idiots at one point. What he is saying is something like this: 'You have been given by God the liberty to shape your life. No power on earth or in the spirit world "owns" you. And now, mysteriously, you seem to want to go backwards. Why? You seem to want to go back to a situation where belonging in the community is conditional on something other than God's act and call. You want to go back to a situation where belonging in the community depends on going through the motions, on some sort of ritual practice: being circumcised, keeping the law. All well and good for the Jewish people, whose heritage this is; but not for you.'

Galatians is famously one of the bits of Paul's work where his temper really seriously runs ahead of him. But he is so irate because he sees people – in effect – wanting to tie not only their own hands but God's – wanting to tell God what he can and can't do. Are you saying, he asks, that to belong to God's people requires the ritual and the law-keeping of the older world of religious practice? If so, do you realize that you're actually trying to lay down terms to God, telling him who he can invite into his company? It's from that kind of conditional, anxious approach to belonging that we have been liberated.

Freedom is the keynote of the letter to Galatia. But of course – and here Paul has to move swiftly to avoid the obvious misunderstanding – this doesn't mean freedom to do what you like. Clearly (and the letter to the Romans bears this out) his remarks on this subject had come back to haunt him. In the first letter to Corinth he has to explain, more than once, that when he and his followers say, 'Everything is lawful now' they don't mean simply that whatever you feel like doing is fine. Twice in 1 Corinthians he refers back to what people have understood him to be saying and hastily corrects it. In 1 Corinthians 6.12: '"I am free to do anything," you say. Yes, but not everything does good. No doubt I am free to do anything, but I for one will not let anything make free with me.' And similarly in 10.23: '"We have the right to do anything," you say? Yes, but not everything builds up the community. You must each of you look after the interests of others, not your own.'

This freedom, in other words, is not a licence to allow our own wonderful, unique, luxuriant personalities to blossom in every possible direction and tread on everyone's toes. The freedom Paul is interested in is something radically different. It is above all a freedom from *thinking that you have to satisfy God before God will welcome you.* That, in Paul's eyes, is the biggest slavery of all: imagining that you have to make God happy before God will invite you in. Get rid of that, Paul is saying, and your slavery is over and the true freedom begins. God is not sitting there, arms folded, waiting for you to entertain him, satisfy him, make him happy and pleased with you. He is already 'pleased' with you in the simple sense that he has decided to invite you and accept you. He is already welcoming you, from all eternity. This is the great theme of the letter to Rome above all – that our relation with God is 'rectified', put straight, justified, as the word is so often translated, by *God's* action calling out *our* trust (not our good behaviour calling out God's approval). The monumentally complex debates about 'justification by faith' as the core of Paul's writing, the debates that shaped so much of the European Reformation, are about what needs to be clarified in order to be sure of giving God the priority in all this. And when the writer to the Ephesians (whether Paul or a close associate) takes this up, what he makes of it is a tremendous, almost mystical, vision. 'Now at last,' he says, 'we have got the point. The penny has dropped. The secret that has been hidden from before the world was created has now been made clear.' And what is that secret? That God is already determinedly and lastingly in love with his Creation. That's the secret, and now it's out there in the plain light of day.

So how exactly does this freedom work? If it's freedom from anxiety about an unknown and unpredictable God, it's freedom from all those behaviours that go with such anxiety – the passionate self-concern that seeks its own security, the fear that others are doing better or are more deeply loved than we are, the search for gratifications of every sort. It is a freedom for new kinds of relationship in which we are at last able to contribute to each other's life and well-being instead of threatening and feeling threatened by each other. So it is also a freedom to bring good news to each other. Christian freedom is the liberty to let God do

God-like things in you – to give life, to promise forgiveness and reconciliation, to communicate hope in word and action.

So it won't do just to say that Christians are liberated from 'law'. They are not subject to the written law in the same way that God's people have been in the past, but this simply means that what that law aimed at is now achieved in other ways, from the inside out, as it were. There is a law 'at work in us', a pattern of regular action – 'the law of Christ'. Paul spells this out in 1 Corinthians 9.21, saying in effect that we are now being 'shaped' by Jesus. When we act and speak, what happens takes on the shape of God in Jesus, the shape of welcome, mercy, service and – in a very particular sense – prayer (about which there'll be more to say in the next chapter). It's crucial for Paul that the freedom we step into, in this brave new world of the Christian community, is *Jesus'* freedom – the kind of life he lived and lives, the relation he has with God the Father, the self-forgetting he shows in his coming among us as human and his sacrificial death. This is what we try to 'imitate' in our lives (see 1 Corinthians 11.1, as well as Philippians 2.5).

This is what it means to say that we have the 'Spirit' of Jesus in us, one of the most dominant ideas in the whole of Paul's writing. This is why Galatians, that great letter on freedom and its challenges, moves towards a reflection in the fifth chapter on just this connection between liberty and the Spirit.

> Be guided by the Spirit and you will not gratify the desires
> of your unspiritual nature . . . Anyone can see the behaviour
> that belongs to the unspiritual nature: fornication, indecency,
> debauchery, idolatry, sorcery, quarrels, contentious tem-
> per, envy, rage, selfish ambition, dissension, party spirit,
> jealousy, drinking bouts, orgies and the rest . . . But the
> harvest of the Spirit is love, joy, peace, patience, kindness,
> goodness, faithfulness, gentleness, self-control.
>
> (Galatians 5.16, 19–21a, 22–23a)

It isn't, after all, completely wrong to say that now I can
do what I like; but the more I am sharing in the Spirit of
Jesus, the more what I 'like', what I desire, is love, joy, peace,
patience and so on. A new pattern has taken hold of me, a
new regularity of behaviour, a new law; the pattern of God's
action in the life and death of Jesus, shared with me, opened
up to me by the 'breathing in' of God's Spirit as it lives in
Jesus.

Another paradox begins to swim into sight in the light of all
this: we're free because now we are 'owned' by Jesus. Paul is
unashamed about this quite provocative language. It is one
of the defining things about Christians that they say 'Jesus
is Lord' (1 Corinthians 12.3); but we need to remember that
in that society, at that time, to say 'Jesus is Lord' was not a
vaguely religious declaration of allegiance. 'Lord', *kurios*, is
a word that means 'owner', 'master', in a way that is not at
all vague or pious. It represents a claim about an ownership

that overrides all others – and in so doing relativizes any possible human claim to 'own' another person. I belong to Jesus, my neighbour belongs to Jesus and my neighbour's neighbour belongs to Jesus. I do not belong to my neighbour and no one belongs to me. I'm not 'owned' by anybody on earth and neither is anyone else – but I *am* owned by Jesus Christ, in the sense that the pattern of his life is now authoritatively shaping mine. This belonging to Jesus frees me from thinking that the constraints of this or any society are identical with the will of God. It is because of this that I can now look at my neighbour with new eyes, with something like awe.

Paul develops this briefly in the letter to Rome, when he is discussing the way Christians pass judgement on each other's behaviour. My respect for my fellow Christian is like my respect for another person's property. I don't walk into my neighbour's house, drop plates on the floor and wipe my boots on the sofa. I respect her property. Well: my Christian neighbour is someone else's property; he or she belongs to Jesus. And so I had better be very careful indeed about behaviour that is the equivalent of dropping him on the floor or wiping my boots on her. My Christian neighbours are precious to someone else: Jesus; precious possessions, jewels in his treasury. I must regard them with the reverence that suggests. Romans chapter 14 has been looking at the various ways in which, then as now, Christians practise that favourite religious hobby of looking down on one another, and Paul spells out the principle in plain terms: 'Those who eat meat must not look down on those who do not. Those who do not eat meat must not pass judgement on those who do. For God has accepted them' (14.3). And then he goes on to make the point about ownership: 'Who are you to pass judgement on someone else's slave? Whether he stands or falls is his master's business. But stand he will. His master has the power to enable him to stand' (14.4). So when you are tempted to look with contempt at the integrity, the piety, the morality, the credibility of your Christian neighbour, just bear in mind that you are interfering with someone else's property, forgetting that this demands that you stand back and act with respect.

Strangely, this rather shocking metaphor of being slaves of Jesus is – as I've already implied – one of the things that begin to make conventional approaches to slavery in the ancient world shift just a bit. People often ask: why didn't St Paul just *denounce* slavery? What was the matter with the early Christians? Couldn't they see that slavery was *wrong*? The short answer is that probably they couldn't in any nice clear modern sense. They were as conditioned to see slavery as normal as we would be conditioned, I suppose, to see our ordinary patterns of social and financial life as normal (what aspects of our current unquestioned assumptions will our grandchildren look back on with the same incredulity as we look back on these attitudes to slavery?). But something is already unsettling them in certain ways; and Paul's little note to his friend Philemon, the shortest of his letters, is one place where this unsettlement comes through clearly. Philemon is a wealthy patron of Paul, whose slave, Onesimus, has apparently run away, causing some kind of financial problem in the process (he may have stolen money or involved his master in some kind of financial embarrassment through a blunder in business arrangements). He's turned up in (presumably) Rome, where Paul is in prison, and he seems, from the way Paul speaks, to have become a Christian believer in Rome, under Paul's guidance. Paul has been con-scripted to write a calming letter to Philemon asking for Onesimus to be taken in again. Bear in mind the rights of life and death exercised by slave owners; Onesimus has a good deal to worry about.

Paul (perhaps with a bit of a sigh, we might imagine) takes up the parchment and the quill, and in his own hand writes a short note to Philemon, squinting at the page, writing probably 'in large letters', as he tells us in another place (Galatians 6.11), because his eyesight is so awful. The gist of the letter is this: you'll perhaps be surprised to hear that our friend Onesimus has just turned up here. I'm sending him back to you; but I'm not sending him back to you just as a slave, but as a fellow believer, as a brother, and I expect you to treat him in that light. Now, I don't want to have to remind you that you owe your salvation to me; I don't want to be in the position of calling in favours. But if you could possibly see your way to doing what I ask and to welcome Onesimus back, I should be very pleased.

It's a vintage piece of Paul: generous, warm and manipulative all at once, and soaked through with a richness of theological understanding.[3] What makes the letter so important is that something very complicated has apparently happened to the simple relation between slave and slave. owner. There is now – from Paul's point of view – a place where one of them is no longer simply a slave, the other no longer simply a slave owner: a place where they look each other in the eye.

About a hundred years after Paul wrote those words two young women, Perpetua and Felicity, faced execution together as Christians in Carthage, one a slave, the other her mistress. They walked into the arena hand in hand to be mauled by the wild animals and eventually dispatched by the executioner's sword. Perpetua owned Felicity; and you didn't, on the whole, walk hand in hand with people you owned. And this little vignette, from the second Christian century, is a reminder of how Paul's language about seeing your neighbour not as belonging to you but as belonging to Jesus began to make a difference. It took centuries for the Church to catch up and put it all together and work out the implications. Not until the Middle Ages do you have people saying quite clearly that (for example) slaves can't be prevented from marrying, or entering a religious order, or even owning property. Not until the eighteenth century do you have a real campaign against slavery. But Paul, whether he realized it or not, was laying the trail, lighting the fuse. Through all those centuries, what you can hear is the fizzing of the powder as it gradually moves towards the great explosion at the end of the eighteenth and the beginning of the nineteenth century, that explosion whose echoes we heard again when we commemorated a few years ago the 200th anniversary of the abolition of the slave trade.

A different kind of community

'Freedom' and 'slavery' are words that Paul weaves into ever more complex patterns. But behind it all is this conviction that there is a space where we can 'look each other in the eye' with both boldness and reverence, knowing that what we see in the neighbour is the person God has welcomed and the person who is 'owned' by Jesus, owned not as a chattel, not as a thing, but because of the creative force within her of the Spirit of Jesus which has taken hold of her. This Spirit shapes who she is and what she does; and it's because of this that the pattern of life in the community is mutual service born of deep attention. That's the imperative underlined so firmly in texts like Romans 15.7, Ephesians 4.32 and many more. And just coming into view here is Paul's most dominant and most original metaphor for all this: belonging in one body – a metaphor he sketches in Romans 12 and develops with great sophistication in 1 Corinthians

12, returning to the theme in Ephesians 4 and, less directly but still powerfully, in 2 Corinthians 8, 9 and 11.

The community of believers, as he understands it, is an organism, in which the welfare of the whole depends on the welfare of every part, where the sickness of any part is the sickness of the whole. Paraphrasing Paul, we could say that when I have a cold, *I* have a cold – not my nose or my throat alone, but I; the whole of my body is involved. Likewise when I am well or happy, *I* am well or happy – not a set of neurons in my brain, but I, a body of flesh and blood with thoughts and feelings. The whole body is benefited when any part flourishes, the whole body is impaired when any part is not flourishing. No bit of the body, you could say, is 'safe' from the rest. We're all liable to be infected by the joy, or the pain, of any part of it.

It has been often and quite rightly noted that metaphors of society as a body can be found in classical literature (and this is echoed in the opening scene of Shakespeare's *Coriolanus*, which is based on an episode related by a Roman historian). But Paul does something new with it. When (as in Shakespeare's play) we hear the rioting workers of Rome being quelled by somebody getting up and giving them a lecture on belonging in one body (a sort of, 'We're all in this together' lecture), the workers of the city are being reminded that they are deeply necessary to the life of the city, just like everybody else, and so they have to pull their weight.

But the difference is marked. You might imagine, in a modern setting, the managing director of a company saying to the lavatory cleaner, 'Of course we couldn't get along without you.' But that would be different from the managing director asking the lavatory cleaner for help or sympathy, saying, 'I need your personal support, not your contracted role.' Different too from the managing director saying to the cleaner, 'Your son's motorbike accident is an issue for all of us; what can we do to support you?' Or from the cleaner saying to the managing director, 'We know how hard your divorce hit you and the family, and we all feel the strain and the loss and want you to know we're thinking of you.' Let alone the managing director saying, 'We need to know from you what you think is fair and unfair in the way this company is run, and we promise to hear you as carefully as any other voice and to act in response.' The metaphor of the body, in other words, becomes something much more dynamic, much more mutual, in Paul's hands. It's not just a matter of 'Everybody's got their part to play, even the lowest and least.' Rather, it is 'Everyone has their *gift to give*. Everyone needs everyone else's gifts and anyone's problem or pain is everyone's problem.' All deserve honour, all deserve protection; this is what it means to recognize that all are animated by the one Spirit of God.

So, moving from this sense of a new belonging and a place where we meet face to face, we are drawn towards a still more intimate model of what it is to be together, a model that has more to do with the life of an animal organism than with an association of separate individuals. Each of us has something the other desperately needs – so that our attitude to one another is not only welcome or service, but also grateful dependence. And once again Paul begins to turn a lot of assumptions upside down. One dramatic example can be found in some of what Paul says about men and women – an area in which he is usually thought to be unenlightened and patriarchal. In 1 Corinthians 7, he's struggling through a whole set of very complicated problems about husbands and wives, about power relations in marriage, about whether it's good to marry or good to refrain from marrying or both. Then, in one of those intriguing throwaway remarks so typical of his great letters, Paul says, 'The wife's body does not belong to her. It belongs to her husband' – a perfectly routine point of view for the period. But he then goes on to add that 'The husband's body doesn't belong to him. It belongs to his wife.' And that is the point at which eyebrows would be raised in any first-century audience, the point of shock. Everybody 'knows' that women belong to men in marriage; but as far as we can tell, no one seems to have suggested before that men belong to women. What is so often most interesting in Paul is not where he reproduces the received wisdom of his culture but where the unsettling newness of the gospel pushes him to a quite new depth of understanding of mutuality. This extraordinary affirmation of *reciprocal* belonging is a strong example of how this works. There is no point in over-emphasizing Paul's radical feminism, given a great deal of what he says elsewhere. But: set that brief remark against the entire social background Paul is speaking out of and it can only be deeply startling.

Paul, we have seen, is busy questioning and transforming assumptions about freedom, belonging and community. And the word he uses for the Christian community, the Church, is *ekklesia*, which is the Greek word for a citizens' assembly: the *ekklesia*, in an ancient Mediterranean city, was a name for the town meeting where you could go and vote if you were a citizen, and debate affairs. So to call a Christian community by this name is to declare that God has called a meeting in which the public affairs of the whole world are at issue, a meeting to which everybody can go, slave, migrant or citizen. In other words, everyone is a citizen here. And in Philippians 3.20, Paul uses another very significant Greek word, *politeuma*. 'Our *politeuma*', he says, 'is in heaven.' Our citizenship, our civic belonging, is not defined by the society we belong to here, but in heaven. We are citizens together of a reality which is not just any bit of this earth, its business and its politics. This citizenship, created by God, is open for all. What God's welcome does is to make us sharers in God's 'city', the place where God's law prevails – which is simply the place where the Spirit of Jesus shapes human lives. What Israel was always designed to be – the place where God's law becomes manifest so that God's character could be visible on earth – the Christian community is, so that Paul in Galatians 6.16 can call the community 'the Israel of God'. Just as Israel in Hebrew Scripture is God's people on pilgrimage, God's people succeeding, failing, serving, sinning, so we are God's people on pilgrimage, but without any ethnic restriction. We, like the Jewish people, are called to display God's character; which doesn't mean, as Paul is careful to say, that God has forgotten his promise to the Jews, simply that for the time being it is our task to carry *their* vocation to every human context. And in chapters 9 to 11 of Romans, he struggles to do justice to the complexities this involves, passionately resisting any idea that the calling of the Jewish people has been 'superseded', pensioned off, while trying to articulate his conviction that this calling has been extended to believers of all ethnic backgrounds. It is a painfully convoluted discussion, and Paul's personal anguish at his own fraught relations with Jews and with many Jewish Christians is much in evidence; but he clings to the hope of a final reconciliation, where the vocations of both Jews and non-Jews are woven together in God's healing purpose.[4]

The healing sacrifice

I spoke in the previous chapter of how in his letter to the Romans Paul is, as it were, turning his head from side to side, saying, 'You think you've got the point? Think again. And [turning rapidly] don't you imagine that because *they* haven't got it, you're any better.' Right at the start of this letter, Paul insists that we must begin by recognizing in the world signs of a system or a complex of processes that has rebelled against its true nature. In spite of God providing plenty of evidence for his love, we seem not to be interested. And he crystallizes that by saying that, in all of this, 'We see the anger of God at work' – meaning by this that as we ignore or try to push back against the love of God, we make our own lives miserable. We make ourselves unable to experience God except as our enemy; this is his 'anger', and it is felt in this way by everybody, the Jew and the Gentile alike. How are we to cope with this? 'If you think you're exempt, think again' is Paul's bleak conclusion (Romans 2.1). What can defend us against this awful pattern of self-destructiveness?

The surprising answer is: God. It is God, and God only, who can defend us against our own refusal to take God seriously. But how do we know this? In Jesus' death, God has sent into the world what St Paul calls (Romans 3.25) a 'propitiation', to use the commonest and most apparently straightforward translation. The original Greek word is in fact quite difficult to translate adequately. It had been used in the Greek version of the Hebrew Scriptures to denote the lid of the Ark of the Covenant in the sanctuary of the Temple, understood as the place where the sacrifices offered to God were mercifully received. If this is right, Paul is saying that the death of Jesus is the place where an offering is made to God *and* accepted by God, thus creating reconciliation between God and the world. And similar sacrificial language is found in many other places in Paul, sometimes connected – as in 1 Corinthians 5.6–8 – with the festival of Passover and the killing of the Passover lamb, whose blood is splashed on the doors of Israelites; sometimes more generally linked with the sacrifices that were made to turn away God's punishment for sin (Romans 8.3). Paul does not have a single 'theory' about this but quite clearly sees the death of Jesus as the supreme peacemaking gift, doing what sacrifice was always meant to do in ancient religious practice, including Judaism. This is an event that makes all well between God and us and between us and our fellow human beings (2 Corinthians 5.18–21; Ephesians 2.11–16; Colossians 1.20).

There is a hymn which declares to God that 'between our sins and their reward / We set the Passion of thy Son, our Lord'.[5] For Paul, it is God who has 'set' the death of Jesus 'between' us and him, so that when he looks at our human world, what he sees, 'covering over' our destructive, miserable, selfish and self-hurting habits, is Jesus' sacrificial suffering and death, an act of unqualified selflessness accepted as the means to heal the hurt and failure of human beings and so a demonstration of love without reservation even for those who do not appear to deserve love (Romans 5.8). Jesus, in whom the life of God is uniquely alive, the embodiment of God's power and wisdom, God's own 'mind', gives himself over completely to the task of reconciliation. The cross shows that God's 'mind' is oriented towards forgiveness, whatever has been done by us. And only the extreme of human violence, the rejection of this divine mind, can make plain how deep our need is, how serious our sickness. For Jesus on behalf of God to take on himself the consequences of that sickness is for him to do what all sacrificial action had always tried to do – to restore a connection or relation that had been broken.

It is not quite – despite long-standing conventional readings of this – that God has required Jesus to take our punishment. This is not what Paul is arguing at this point. It is more that God, through the life and death and resurrection of Jesus, has brought into the world what he himself most deeply is – selfless love; and thus has made possible a relation with himself that was not possible before. He has shown that he will see in us *what we can be transformed into*, seeing the future he himself desires to bring about in his act of new creation – and shown that he will bring this about by breathing into us the energy of Jesus' Spirit, making us belong in and to him in Christ. And this is the theme that carries forward the next section of the letter to Rome as it moves towards a moment of climax in chapter 8, where Paul gives us one of his most wonderful and eloquent pictures of the world's possible future. The world is tormented by frustration; it can't be what it was meant to be, it is struggling and groaning. And yet something is struggling to *burst out of it*, to come to birth. Such is the force of this that, once we recognize what is seeking to be born in and from us – the life of Jesus – our old habits have no claim on us. We aren't obliged to live in the destructiveness and selfishness we are used to. If we do so, we simply die – there is no truthful and creative life for us in this world or any other. But if, by the Spirit that is pushing in us to be fully born, we see to it that what dies is the whole world of selfish, destructive habit, we shall live, here and hereafter, and live in a relation to God that is like that of Jesus.

> All who are led by the Spirit of God are children of God. And the spirit you have received is not a spirit of slavery, leading you back into fear, but the spirit of adoption, enabling us to cry, 'Abba, Father', the Spirit affirming to our spirit that we are God's children.   (Romans 8.14–15)

The Spirit prays in us with the same words Jesus used (as St Mark's Gospel tells us) in the Garden of Gethsemane on the night before he died.

But Paul goes on to extend this picture of something transforming being brought to birth to the whole of the universe: everywhere we see one or another kind of frustration, everywhere it seems that the purposes of creation are being turned back on themselves. And yet, in us, in the community of belief, the Spirit is stirring; in us the relationship between Creator and creature has been healed. So in us hope for the whole Creation becomes visible and credible (Romans

8.19–25). There will be more to say about this extraordinary passage in the next chapter, but what matters for now is to see how the whole logic of the great letter to the Romans rests on this as its focal point. Paul's vision is about more than simply the overcoming of the division or polarity between Jew and non-Jew, more than simply freedom from the slavery of fear. It's about a renewal of all that exists, about something entirely fresh coming to birth, bridging the gap between God and what isn't God.

And we, who have taken the step of trust that brings us together into the open space cleared by the love of God, where we see each other face to face – we, God help us, are in the middle of the story. We represent the hope of the universe: which should make us sit up sharply. We are delivered from slavery and empowered to pray in a new way, Jesus' way; we are given the strength to live in service and attention and welcome to one another; and the whole long-term point of it all is so that the whole universe may see hope coming to birth.

As Paul repeats time and again, all this is to do with God and not us (see, for example, 2 Corinthians 4.7). The new world does not come into being because we are brilliant, holy, loving and reconciling, because we're not. But God is; and anything that happens to bring this newness into the world is God's work, from first to last. Paul regularly reminds his hearers that there is no ground for boasting, nothing to be pleased with ourselves about. We are not to waste time feeling pleased with ourselves; our time must be given to thanking God.

But when things are going really badly, when we have no inclination to feel too pleased with ourselves, then too we need to thank God. Because it is when things are going really badly that we know absolutely for a fact that the triumph of grace has nothing to do with us. Our failure, our struggle, our abject mess, can be good news. After all, if we were all brilliant and successful, handsome, eloquent and saintly, people might run away with the idea that it was us rather than God making the difference. There is a certain wryness to the way Paul treats this: rubbing his infected eyes, smoothing his balding head, straightening his stooping back and wishing he was half a foot taller, he can say ruefully that at least no one could confuse the effect of his preaching with the force and attractiveness of his physical presence (1 Corinthians 2.1–5; compare Galatians 4.14 and 2 Corinthians 10). In the long apologia he gives in 2 Corinthians 10–12, Paul poignantly details not only the sufferings he has faced for the sake of his mission but the humiliations he has faced; and he makes no secret of the profound pain he feels at the criticism he receives, the patronizing attitude of some of his rivals or enemies. So when he deprecates his own skill and attractiveness, when he reminds us in 1 Corinthians 2 that he's actually not a particularly good speaker, or in Galatians 4.14 that he must have looked a sorry sight when he first preached in the region, what he is saying is that what's going on in the life of the Christian assembly is not just a turning upside down of social status and community structure, but a turning upside down of everything we think about success and prosperity and about the images of ourselves we want to cultivate.

Paul, in short, is revaluing, rethinking the whole universe he lives in, not only the social but the physical universe, moving us into a comprehensive new frame of reference. He is seeking to help us see what a universe might look like in which the welcoming acceptance of God had become visible and effective in a unique new way through the life and death and resurrection of Jesus, understood as a set of events that radically cleared away our fear of God and our avoidance both of his love and of his demands. And as we shall see in our final chapter, this ultimately requires from us a rethinking of what can be said about God himself.

3

The new creation:
Paul's Christian universe

Their unbelieving minds are so blinded by the God of this passing age, that the gospel of the glory of Christ who is the image of God cannot dawn upon them and bring them light.   (2 Corinthians 4.4)

The image of God in Jesus

Let's begin with that deceptively simple phrase 'the image of God' – because in trying to understand how, for Paul, the whole universe is reorganized around the figure of Jesus, this idea is central. But it is essential to remember how very strange such a phrase would have been when first uttered. As noted in our first chapter, Paul is roughly the same age as Jesus, perhaps a few years younger; and twenty or so years after Jesus' execution, Paul is saying that this person, his contemporary, somebody who was well known to people that Paul knew well, is the image of God – that in him, as he just as startlingly puts it in 1 Corinthians 1.24, is the power and wisdom of God; or that – as he says in 2 Corinthians 4.4–6 – in his face shines the glory of God, what the Jews called the *shekhinah*, the blinding radiance of God's presence. In Hebrew Scripture, this presence is described as radiating so powerfully that it throws people to the ground; it's like a dense fog of light which you can't breathe in and you can't stand in (1 Kings 8.10–11, where the glory comes down on the newly consecrated Temple in Jerusalem and the priests cannot stay on their feet to do their work).

And that glory, that stifling intensity of presence in holy places, is what you see and sense if you look at Jesus, so Paul claims: a strong claim, to put it mildly. Imagine for a moment what a leap of imagination would be involved in thinking of someone of your own generation and background in terms like that.

So in this chapter what I hope to do is to unpick a little of the process by which Paul comes to that kind of conclusion, and the ways in which he works it out so as to make it a shaping, a dictating element for human life. And as I hinted in the previous chapter, part of the answer to that question can be found in the character of Paul's conversion as he and others tell us about it. On the road to Damascus – where he is about to arrest members of the Christian group and take them back for punishment, perhaps even lynching, in Jerusalem – he is surrounded and overtaken by 'glory', surrounded by choking, blinding light, so intense that it knocks him off his horse. He can't see because of the intensity of the light; he is literally blinded for a few days. And from the heart of this blinding, stifling, overwhelming radiance a voice speaks and a human face emerges: the face of the Galilean rebel executed in humiliating circumstances some two or three years earlier, to the satisfaction of Paul's priestly patrons. This experience is at the heart of so much of what Paul later unfolds in his theology. Here is the radiance of God speaking with the voice of Jesus; and even more than that, the voice challenges the young Saul with the words, 'Why are you persecuting me?' Not, 'Why are you persecuting my friends?' This is not just a vision of an individual dead man who is somehow mysteriously alive with God; it is a vision of someone in whose life the lives and sufferings of his friends and associates are entirely bound up. From the earliest days of Christianity, Paul's readers have seen in these words the root of Paul's understanding of Jesus as having a living body on this earth in the lives of his followers, those human beings who are united with him by the breath of his Spirit.

Bear in mind this visionary theme and then turn for a moment to the other pole of Paul's thinking, the theme we find especially in the third chapter of his letter to the church in Galatia. Here he picks up what must have been one of the most difficult things for him and his colleagues. Jesus died by *crucifixion*; not only did he die in an agonizing and intensely humiliating way, 'Suffering in a public place / A death reserved for slaves', as W. H. Auden puts it in one of his poems;[6] he died in a way that, according to the Jewish law, placed him under a curse. The law of Moses states

61

(Deuteronomy 21.22–23) that the body of an executed criminal exposed to be hanged or impaled on a tree or stake is accursed, something that pollutes the land (which is why it must not be left hanging overnight). As commentators note, this humiliation is reserved for those who have in some way threatened the very existence of God's people (Joshua 8.29, 10.26; 1 Samuel 31.10; Esther 9.6–14).[7] So Paul's claim is potentially very shocking indeed. This executed body hanged on a tree, instead of being unclean, something to be thrown out, an object of God's enmity, is what speaks of how God includes everyone and everything and overcomes enmity. Something of the same argument is behind the strange statement in 2 Corinthians 5.21 that God has 'made him [Jesus] to be sin for us': Jesus has taken on the appearance of a universal scapegoat, the thing everyone rejects and throws out, symbolizing all that is opposed to God; in his suffering, he sums up the very essence of abandonment, Godlessness, the fate of human beings left to themselves. But because he does so as the one who acts on behalf of God in the world, this shouldering of the burden of our estrangement from God becomes the supreme good news: no abandonment is too deep or dark for God to penetrate and heal.

We could say that Paul is, as it were, working inwards from both ends of a very long spectrum – at one end, Jesus as the one who carries the intensity of God's glory; at the other, Jesus as the one who represents what is most dramatically estranged from God. Paul's Jesus is a figure who immediately presents us with the sharpest of contradictions, and it takes all of Paul's great conceptual and imaginative brilliance to show his readers how this picture does not fall apart. If Jesus is indeed the bearer of 'glory', he must in some sense stand above and beyond the categories of the law of Moses. If Jesus is – in the terms of Roman and Judaean politics and power at the time – the most comprehensively humiliated and despicable figure imaginable, the glory of God cannot be simply a hugely inflated version of human success, glamour or security. Put all this together, and you may begin to see how Paul's thinking about Jesus, his thinking about what characterizes the Christian community, his thinking about freedom and law, appear all of a piece. The argument gathers gradually: if Jesus is involved in the lives and sufferings of his people ('Why are you persecuting me?'), he must be more than merely an individual figure from the past; if Jesus appears as the one in whom God's radiant presence can be sensed as powerfully as in the Temple of Jerusalem, he is one who carries God's glory into the heart of human suffering; if Jesus is an executed criminal of the kind representing ultimate hostility to God or alienation from God, then something has historically gone wrong with how we human beings conceive both God and human power. In the light of all this, what is it that now has to change in the way we think about God?

One way of reading Paul's letters is as a series of attempts to answer that question, and to answer it in relation to what needs to be said about Jesus. If all of what has just been said is valid, it is not going to be enough to say that he is a great prophet, a great teacher from the past; and Paul inches his way towards thinking the unthinkable. If this is where the radiance of God is seen, where the power of God is felt, where the wisdom of God is learned, this is where God is. To speak truthfully about God now involves us in speaking about Jesus.

It's possible that already in the ninth chapter of the letter to the Romans (9.5), Paul has come to a place where he can explicitly call Jesus God; but there is much debate about the text. It comes at the end of a long discussion about the destiny of the Jewish people and it reads literally as follows:

> They are Israelites, of whom is the adoption and the glory and the covenants and the law and the worship and the promises, of whom the patriarchs, and of whom the Messiah according to the flesh, God above all, blessed for ever.

Greek manuscripts don't punctuate; so what is Paul saying? 'From them by natural descent came the Messiah who is God over all, blessed for ever'? Or 'From them by natural descent came the Messiah; and may God who is over all be blessed for ever'? The translations vary and we cannot be certain – though most interpreters prefer the latter option. But whatever conclusion we come to about this passage, there is no doubt at all, as we have seen already, of what he wants to say in 1 Corinthians 1 and 2 Corinthians 4: Jesus is the place where the presence and power of God are seen to reside. He is associated with some of the most resonant and evocative language you find in Hebrew Scripture, the language of glory and wisdom – both ways of speaking about how God impinges directly on the world here and now.

So when we move on to the three prison letters, Ephesians, Colossians and Philippians, we see there the natural next step being taken. In Colossians we read that God

> rescued us from the domain of darkness and brought us into the kingdom of his dear Son. He is the image of the invisible God. He is the firstborn of all creation, and in him everything in heaven and on earth is created, things visible and the invisible orders of thrones, sovereignties, authorities and powers. The whole universe has been created through him and for him. He is before all things and all things find coherence in him.

If Jesus is indeed the place where the power and radiance of God may be seen, then in him is the power, the energy, that sustains all things and gives coherence to all things. The same point is echoed in Philippians 2, in the famous hymn of Christ's humility, where we are told that Jesus is 'in the form of God'. And we find it in the great first chapter of Ephesians, in one of the longest sentences in the whole of the Bible: here we are told that in Christ everything finds its unity, so that the entire universe, 'everything in heaven and earth', is to be brought into unity in Christ. Even if there is still debate about who wrote some of these texts in their present form, it should be clear enough that the thinking in them is deeply in tune with what Paul is already saying in Romans and Galatians and the letters to Corinth. 'Everything has its destiny in union with Jesus Christ'; or, as we might put it in plainer terms, everything *makes sense* because of Jesus: not just human life, but the life of the entire universe. And this is so because he is the face of God turned towards what is not God; he reveals to us a God who moves out into engagement with what he is not – in creation itself, in reconciling love, in welcome (to use once again that crucial category). That is the God in whom we believe; and because of believing in that God everything hangs together.

Why is there a world? Because God is that kind of God. Why are we able to give thanks to God? Because God is that kind of God. Why can we be confident that we have reconciliation and absolution for our failures and sins? Because God is that kind of God, the God whose form and face we see in Jesus. Everything hangs together because of this. In the fifteenth chapter of the first letter to the Corinthians, we see Paul drawing all this together in a picture of the very end of time, when Jesus sweeps up everything together into one great ensemble and presents it to God the Father; as if the Son of God has travelled around the whole span of reality, collected it all together and brought it back to his Father as a gift, a treasure.

The image of God in us

But there's more to it, because of course what St Paul is evoking is not a Jesus who simply sits on the throne of heaven and receives our prayers, but a Jesus who – because his own life in time and eternity consists entirely in pouring out praise and love to God the Father – continually sweeps us up into his activity. In his lifetime, the Gospels tell us, Jesus prays, and when he prays he says, 'Abba, Father'. He is the power and glory of God – yet he turns to an Other, to the mysterious source that he calls his Father. And, says Paul, when he prays in love, attention, delight, trust towards God his Father, we are caught up in the 'slipstream' of that great energy driving towards the Father from Christ.

As we noted earlier, Paul spells this out clearly in Romans 8.15 and Galatians 4.6. The Spirit of God comes alive in us so that we are able to say Jesus' own words, 'Abba, Father', the simple Aramaic address of Jesus to the source of his life and identity. We are able to speak Jesus' words to God, as if we were, like Jesus, directly connected to God as God's children – sons and daughters of God, because of the gift of the eternal Son of God, the eternal issuing-forth from God that is power, wisdom, glory, the divine Son embodied in Jesus Christ. Thus the same agency that distributes gifts in the Church, the same agency that binds us to one another in respect and love and service, is what gives us the courage to say, 'Abba, Father'. Paul more than once in his letters (as in 2 Corinthians 3.12 and Ephesians 3.12) uses the word *parrhesia* to describe the spirit in which we are to approach God: it is a word that means 'boldness' – almost 'nerve'; it is the freedom to say openly what we want to. And our readiness to come to God with the words of Jesus on our lips is very naturally seen as a case of this 'boldness' – as we are reminded in the formula often used at the Eucharist to introduce the Lord's Prayer: 'As our Saviour Christ has commanded and taught us, we are bold to say . . .' We have the nerve to call God what Jesus called him, because of the Spirit we share with Jesus as a result of being baptized, 'immersed' in the life of Jesus (e.g. 1 Corinthians 12.13–14), buried with him as he dies so that we may come alive afresh in him (Romans 6.3–4).

This makes it clear that Paul's teaching about God, Christ and the Spirit is closely bound up with his understanding of the continuing Christian experience of *prayer*. If, mysteriously, we are given the courage to say 'Father' to the indescribable source of all things, if we are able to treat as 'family' the one for whom we can find no adequate words or images, this starts off a train of thought that leads to radically new understandings of how to speak not only to but also *about* God. As the Spirit gives us the words of Jesus to speak and creates among us something of the self-giving, attentive, patient and delighted love that Jesus shares with Father and Spirit, we can rightly say that the divine life is appearing on earth; and that life is shown to be a life in which mutuality is an eternal fact. Paul is already working with a 'Trinitarian' view of God, even if the concepts have not yet been fully formulated. And the way he puts it also means that in an important sense we are already *in the future*: God's future is alive here and now, and it is us. We who are living in the Christian community are living *on the other side of the end of the world*, living in God's life – to which the whole life of the universe is being drawn, not in an irresistible natural process but by a timeless and unchanging love seeking to reconcile or heal what is broken in the created world at every level.

Turn back here to the eighth chapter of Romans. Paul says,

> You live by the Spirit, since God's Spirit dwells in you; anyone who does not possess the Spirit of Christ does not belong to Christ. But if Christ is in you then although the body is dead because of sin, yet the Spirit is your life because you have been declared righteous. If the Spirit of him who raised Jesus from the dead is living in you then the God who raised Christ Jesus from the dead will give new life to your mortal bodies from his indwelling Spirit. (Romans 8.9–11)

And, a little later (8.16–17, 22–23):

> The Spirit of God affirms to our spirit that we are God's
> children, and if children then heirs, heirs of God, fellow heirs
> with Christ; but we must share his sufferings if we are also
> to share his glory. Up to the present, as we know, the whole
> created universe and all its parts groans as if in the pangs of
> childbirth. What is more, we also to whom the Spirit is given
> as the first fruits of the harvest to come are groaning inwardly
> as we look forward eagerly to our adoption, our liberation
> from mortality.

The Spirit brings the first fruits of the harvest, the beginning
of everlasting life; it begins here and now – which is why we
can say that the end of the world is in one sense over and
done with for the person who lives in Jesus. We are on the
far side of all that; we are already experiencing a 'foretaste',
an advance sample of the experience God has made us for,
the experience of mutual love and contemplative joy in his
presence. In 2 Corinthians 1.22 and Ephesians 1.13, Paul
uses the Greek word *arrabon*, a 'down-payment', to describe
this 'advance' experience, this foretaste of the future; for him,
the life of the body of Christ, the Christian community, is
life in heaven.

Whatever else he is, Paul is a realist; we shouldn't give way
to the temptation to think that language like this shows
him to have been a deluded dreamer. The real Church is

that place where people are persistently and faithfully serving one another, anxiously and passionately striving for the welfare of their neighbour, soaked through with the joy of a future already experienced that is a share in the eternal Son's joyful gazing at the Father. It is also a place where people are torn apart with compassion at the failure and sin of others, ready to suffer and endure anything so that those sins and sufferings may be healed. When all that is operative, there is a foretaste of heaven in a community defined by a level of generosity we can only think of as divine. If we never saw any of that in the Church we might very rightly give up on it.

But Paul knows perfectly well that the congregations he knows are not uniformly and consistently 'heavenly', any more than the ones we know; look at what he has to say about the disorderly and quarrelsome communities in Corinth. Yet he can make these extraordinary claims about the Church as embodying God's future because running through the life of these frail human groups like a steady, relentless stream is the reality of mutual love and delight that is God's life. However energetically we try and fill the stream up with mud, it keeps flowing through because it is driven on by the Spirit. I can't resist mentioning here something I heard many years ago from a distinguished senior bishop of the Church of England who had been brought up in a very strict Protestant sect. When he began to study the Bible seriously as a teenager and to read 1 Corinthians, he was surprised to discover that the Church of the Bible was apparently full of greedy, lecherous, drunken, disreputable characters, who needed the stern words of St Paul to bring them into line. And having recognized the nature of the biblical Church, he duly decided to join the Church of England . . . Not a completely serious defence of the C of E, perhaps. But it underlines the point that what matters about the Church is less our achievement than God's gift. It is when we look at the gift that we see what it means to think of the Church as heaven on earth, a human group caught up into the action of God.

It may be to go a little beyond what St Paul explicitly says, but we can grasp in this light why many Christians speak of the Church's worship as 'heaven on earth', especially the Lord's Supper, the Eucharist. Eastern Orthodox Christians typically insist that the worship of the Church is the presence of heaven on earth; and in doing so they are entirely in tune with what St Paul wants to say about the Church's life as a whole. It makes perfect sense that this 'heaven on earth' character should be most marked when what is happening is the sacramental celebration of God's action, when we are seeking to be as open and transparent as we can be to what God is doing. The Eucharist is where the body of Jesus that is the community of believers opens its hands to receive the body of Jesus that is the bread blessed in his name; and that moment where the body renews itself by feeding on the body, where one kind of presence is energized afresh by another, that moment is indeed 'heavenly', a showing forth of what renewed humanity is and will be.

Christ is the presence of the fullness of glory, the end of time, the Creation at peace with itself and God; and so Christ is also the restoration of authentic humanity – the fullness of humanity as well as the fullness of divinity. There are two texts that we can read alongside each other on this. Colossians 2.9 proclaims that 'It is in Christ that the Godhead in all its fullness dwells embodied and it is in him that you have been brought to fulfilment'. And Ephesians 4.13 looks forward to the point when 'we all attain to the unity inherent in our faith and in our knowledge of the Son of God, to mature humanity measured by nothing less than the full stature of Christ'. Full divinity and mature humanity are shown inseparably in Jesus; and the Church where the Spirit lives, the Church where the future is already experienced, where heaven is at work, is the place where we can see what we most need to know about God – but also, crucially, what we need to know about human beings. What does humanity look like in its depth, in its maturity? Look at a life lived in relation to Jesus and you'll see. Where do we find the fullness of the work of God, so fully that we can't find words for it? Look in the Church and see what its worship means, says and does. That fullness of both divine and human life is there together in the body of Christ on earth – the body that hung on the cross, accursed and humiliated, the body that is now the community breaking bread. It is because of

73

this that we can think of the whole world being welcome in one community: the true depth of human identity and destiny is there in Jesus, and so any and every human person can find himself or herself in relation to him (whether here and now they know it or not).

I mentioned earlier that Paul is a 'Trinitarian' thinker, even though he does not use this vocabulary. What we have been trying to trace is how, in these letters written so very early in the Christian story, we see the life of God being imagined all over again as a life of gift and mutuality and delight – in Jesus, in the one he calls Father, in the energy or 'breath' that flows from him. It's not the language of the Nicene Creed; but, as with so much in the Gospel and the letters of John, the same pattern emerges, the threefold life of gift and self-sharing. If we can say that the life of Jesus becomes the 'law' of the new community, this comes to the same thing as saying that the life of the threefold God becomes the law of Christians. And when Paul approaches questions of ethics, what is uppermost in his mind is not how to clarify a set of moral principles, rules or values so much as how to understand our habits and decisions in the light of whether or not they communicate this law of life – the divine 'style' of living and relating. It is very important to locate what St Paul says about the moral life against this background. Paul, like his great interpreter St Augustine, has a bad name as a moralist: everyone thinks they know what Paul was against – from homosexuality to women not wearing hats in church, and perhaps some vague memory of a text about the love of money being the root of all evil (1 Timothy 6.10).

But read Paul's letters carefully and it is clear enough that morality for him is about *manifestation*. A good life is a life that *shows* something; that shows 'glory', shows the delight, the service, the attention, the generosity that God has made to dwell in the community. A good life is simply a life that shows what the body of Christ is like, which is why Paul can say (as we have noted) that it's all very well to say everything is permitted, but not everything builds up the common life. The key question is what continues to build us up so that we reflect and make visible the generosity of God (see, for example, 2 Corinthians 8 and 9, especially 9.11, where the point of human generosity is understood as to provoke gratitude to God). This is where we begin to answer questions about what's good and what's bad – not in abstract terms but in the very concrete language of life and death, of wholeness and sickness or dysfunction. Paul can be crystal clear about the kinds of behaviour which immediately suggest to him a kind of sickness, a failure to live in the Spirit (see for example 1 Corinthians 6.9–10 and Galatians 5.19–21). He is not arguing for a sentimental morality with no boundaries and lots of excuses. But we need to see what makes unacceptable behaviour unacceptable; and it is fundamentally the way it pulls against Spirit-led mutuality, that humility before the other to which Paul returns again and again. Sometimes we can clearly see the connection, as when Paul speaks about unbalanced greed, party spirit, sexual rapacity; sometimes it is not quite so instantly clear. But what matters is the principle from which he argues, the principle of nourishing the common life of mutual gift – which is ultimately the divine life lived on earth.

Remember the overriding theme of the letter to the Romans, with its repeated insistence on undermining *everybody's* self-righteousness. You think you're better than your neighbour? Think again. You as a Jew think you're better than your Gentile neighbour? Think again. You as a Gentile think you're better than your Jewish neighbour? Think again. You believe that as a careful and precise rigorist, seeking the maximum strictness and consistency of behaviour, you are more pleasing to God? You pride yourself on your free-spirited, generous, adventurous liberalism, so different from the sour legalism of your neighbour? Whatever point of advantage you have been trying to establish has to be dissolved; you must start again from the vision of Spirit-led mutuality, working out how the body is built up and the life of God made manifest. The good is what serves the community, not this or that individual's self-image. But this is not a serving of the community that overrides the dignity of the unique person. On the contrary, what is good is what gives life to each and all, what liberates each person to give what only he or she can to the common life. Here, 1 Corinthians 8 and Romans 14.13 following are very significant passages, in that they spell out the way in which Christian giving is not a

matter of haves being kind to have-nots but of all recognizing that they depend on each other. And the Romans text is
a powerful reiteration of Paul's impatience with the search
in the community for a position of ultimate moral–spiritual
high ground; disputes between rigorists and more accom-
modating believers are a waste of time if the only thing worth
looking at is how my action makes for the well-being and
integrity of my neighbour.

The same thing lies behind Paul's remarks in Colossians 2,
where he is very critical of excessive asceticism, unbalanced
'self-denial'. Once again, Paul is challenging the impulse to
find a superior position: if you're engaging in self-denial
as a way of self-assertion – and some people do – beware.
Despising the physical body is no part of Paul's ethics. But
he is sometimes thought of as teaching this, partly because
of misunderstandings about the way he uses the language of
'flesh' and 'spirit'. A passage like Romans 8.5–8 contrasting
those who live 'according to the flesh' and 'according to the
spirit' is a case in point. But when Paul speaks of 'flesh' in
such a connection, he is talking about the whole of human
life seen from one point of view – the point of view of
mutual exclusion. Living in or by the flesh is living as though
the world were composed of hard lumps of stuff bumping
up against each other. Flesh, after all, is stuff you can't actually put your hands through, stuff that isn't transparent or
porous, stuff that bumps into other stuff. So life in the flesh
is the life of people who are closed off from one another,

while life in the spirit is the life of people who are opened up to one another. This is very clear when Paul catalogues the sort of behaviour that belongs to 'the flesh' in the fifth chapter of the letter to Galatia. He begins with what sounds like a series of obviously physical disorders, fornication, indecency and debauchery; then moves on a little to idolatry and sorcery. We might imagine some enthusiastic listeners nodding at the story so far: yes, fornication is very bad; yes, idolatry, can't have that. But then he moves on to quarrels, contentious temper, envy, fits of rage, selfish ambition, dissension . . . and perhaps some of the enthusiasts who have been nodding might begin to wonder. It's pretty plain that flesh is human life seen from the point of view of people bumping into each other, treading on each other's toes, competing for space: lives closed off from each other. And spirit, which involves love, joy, peace, patience, kindness, goodness, fidelity and so on, does not relate to a set of internal 'values' or some such, but to clearly visible *physical* behaviours. Spirit in Paul, whether with a small 's' or a capital, is not a vague inspirational force floating several feet above ground; it is what makes you practically generous and sympathetic to your neighbour; very prosaic.

John Crook, a very wise Ch'an Buddhist master who died recently, left a collection of brief meditations, in one of which he describes an encounter with his own spiritual teacher, where he poured out a number of elevated thoughts and aspirations about enlightenment and so on. His master, he said, looked at him in silence for a long time, then sighed and said, 'John, when were you last kind?' It is very close to Paul's down-to-earth account of 'spirit'; the irony is that it is the 'flesh' that is the unreal and evaporating world, because that picture of competing and clashing solid bodies is a fictional account of the actual world we live in, where bodies are the means of communication and love, inseparable from the life of spirit. The spiritual is the realistic.

Living in the new creation

In 2 Corinthians 5.17, Paul says that to be baptized in commitment to Jesus is to become or to be involved in a 'new creation'. Everything is beginning again because the real universe (as distinct from the fantasy world of our fear, selfishness, greed, folly and rivalry) is the universe that hangs together finally because of the love of Jesus. We are living in that new creation, that radically different universe: the new city with its new citizenship, where no one is a slave or migrant deprived of dignity, where we live here and now, but at the same time in the living presence of the future. What is coming, what is going to flower and develop in the future, is here already. We are living in the overlap between the present and the future, between two worlds, beyond the constraints and injustices of the present social order.

Paul, of course, looks forward to the second coming of Jesus Christ; and in his very early letters, he seems to think of this pretty literally. The first and second letters to the church in Thessalonica (generally thought to be among the earliest written) have pictures of a glorified Jesus descending from heaven with trumpets, clouds and angels, and the faithful being swept up from the earth into the air, while the spiritual enemies of Jesus are destroyed by the revelation of his glory. This is the picture that has been set in concrete by certain kinds of American fundamentalists who talk about the 'rapture'. But Paul moved on: we can see something of that moving on in his great meditation on the resurrection in 1 Corinthians 15. There is still a dramatic picture: 'the trumpet will sound and the dead will be raised incorruptible, and we shall be changed'. But all of this is simply one facet of the great universal climax of Christ bringing the whole world back home to its source.

This is the universe's destiny. And by the time we get to Ephesians, Philippians and Colossians, the 'prison letters', there's relatively little about the end of the world and a great deal about what I earlier described as the Christian experience of living *now* on the other side of the end of the world. The hope, the delight, of the end is seeping through, penetrating, the whole of our present life. Yes, Christ has died, Christ is risen, Christ will come again; I don't think that Paul changed his mind about the future hope of Christ returning in glory. But his interest seems more and more to be in how we experience now the life that Christ will give in fullness at the end of time. And in such a perspective, the end is something like the world blossoming into its fullness under the hand of Christ, until finally the history of the world and the presence of Christ come together at the end of all things.

In Philippians 3.13, Paul talks about being 'stretched out in longing' towards what lies ahead, forgetting what's behind; yearning for the fullness that is already beginning to germinate in the present moment. He longs for Christ's future, but it is because he has already begun to sense it in the present. This was a passage that played a very significant part in early Christian thinking and praying, and is perhaps one of the most important legacies of Paul's vision. As we begin to mature as Christians, there is a dawning awareness that our hope in Christ is not just about a future event. It's about a future that has already started, manifest in our relation to one another, to Jesus and to the One whom Jesus calls, 'Abba, Father'. It is the life of God the Trinity opening up to us and living itself out in our lives – in the present moment, yes; but in a way that lets us know that it will go on growing into a depth for which we cannot find words or pictures – 'the depth of the riches of the wisdom and knowledge of God' (Romans 11.33).

Questions for reflection or group discussion

1 Outsiders and insiders: Paul's social world

1 Who are our modern-day 'citizens' (those with full rights and status), 'outsiders' (those who 'half-belong' in our society) and 'slaves' (those with few rights)?

2 How socially diverse is your own local Christian community? Does it matter?

3 Does the question of knowing who is 'in' and who is 'out' matter for the Church? If not, why not? And, if so, on what basis do we make this distinction?

4 What about Paul's personality do you find compelling? Or off-putting? How does it feel to know that Paul might have suffered from a disability?

5 'What Paul preached was not a new "religion" ... it was a new world order.' What are your reactions to this statement?

2 The universal welcome: Paul's disturbing idea

1 When was the last time you felt welcomed? What was that like?

2 How can you, your family or your church demonstrate the kind of 'universal welcome' described here, breaking down barriers between people? Would other people find this disturbing? Would *we* be disturbed?

3 How would you define 'freedom'? What misunderstandings of this word do you see in the world around us?

4 How does it feel to know that God welcomes you, that you belong and that you are free from having to earn that welcome?

5 Is slavery completely 'abolished' in our world? If not, what modern forms of slavery persist and how can we pray and work against them?

3 The new creation: Paul's Christian universe

1 What do you think about the idea that the death of Jesus somehow shows us the 'image of God'? Is this the image of God we expect?

2 Because of Jesus' death, we have been welcomed into relationship with God so that we can boldly say 'Abba, Father'. How does that feel?

3 Paul places a lot of emphasis on the idea of 'union with Christ' or of being 'in Christ' – what is your understanding of this idea?

4 What do you make of the distinction between 'living by the flesh' and 'living by the Spirit'? Reflect on any examples of 'fleshly' living in your own life, and ask yourself what you can do to live more 'spiritually' (remembering how that word is defined in this chapter).

5 The Church is called to be 'heaven on earth', the down-payment on God's future, living in the overlap between this world and the world to come. How does this feel and what might this look like?

Lenten reading guide

Week one

Ash Wednesday:	Acts 7.54—8.3
Thursday:	Acts 9.1–31
Friday:	Acts 16.16–40
Saturday:	Acts 17.1–34

Sunday reflection

Saul of Tarsus was once staunchly committed to maintaining the boundary between those who were 'inside' and those who were 'outside'. He was a zealous defender of the letter of the law and a persecutor of the Church. Until, that is, he met Jesus on the Damascus road — then everything changed! Saul the persecutor became Paul the apostle, and went from one who wreaked havoc on the Church to preaching the message that Jesus was the Messiah, and that God was now tearing down the wall of hostility between Jews and Gentiles, a wall he once worked hard to build up. Are we prepared for our encounter with Jesus to challenge us, and possibly to radically change us?

Father, in this season of Lent, help us to see Jesus and, as we see him, to be deeply changed, as you changed Paul. Help us to become people who pray and work against unjust exclusion and against all walls that separate your people in your Church and in our society. Amen.

Week two

Monday:	2 Cor. 10.1–18
Tuesday:	2 Cor. 11.1–15
Wednesday:	2 Cor. 11.16–30
Thursday:	Phil. 2.1–11
Friday:	Phil. 2.12–30
Saturday:	Phil. 3.1–11

Sunday reflection

As a well-educated Jewish man with Roman citizenship, Paul once enjoyed status and privilege. But he powerfully declares all this 'rubbish' in the light of the good news of Jesus Christ. Why? Because Paul recognized that he followed a King who surrendered his privileges, became a slave and died a shameful death. What privileges do we enjoy? Can we, like Paul, 'count them as loss'?

Lord Jesus, in this Lenten season, help us to consider all our privileges to be rubbish, that we may gain you and be found in you. Amen.

Week three

Monday:	Eph. 2.1–10
Tuesday:	Eph. 2.11–22
Wednesday:	Eph. 3.1–20
Thursday:	Rom. 14.1–12
Friday:	Rom. 14.13–23
Saturday:	Rom. 15.1–7

Sunday reflection

Unity is relatively easy if you close the doors and keep out those who think differently. Likewise, being welcoming is relatively easy if you give up on unity. The hard thing, and the thing that Paul cared deeply about and strove to instil in his churches, is to do both at once: to be united as one body but also profoundly welcoming to the outsider. How might we try to do this in our lives, our communities and in the Church?

Father, thank you for welcoming us. Help us, and help your Church, increasingly to become a place where there is a welcome for all and where there is unity. Amen.

Week four

Monday:	Philemon 1–25
Tuesday:	1 Cor. 8.1–13
Wednesday:	1 Cor. 9.1–14
Thursday:	1 Cor. 10.23–33
Friday:	Gal. 4.21–31
Saturday:	Gal. 5.1–15

Sunday reflection

The message of freedom is at the heart of Paul's gospel. He may not have expressed opposition to slavery in the way we might want him to, but his message of a new people, formed by the gospel, challenged the social systems of slavery at their core. Today we rejoice that institutional slavery has long been abolished, but we are also aware that it continues, in other forms, both abroad and at home. What might the gospel have to say to these modern forms of slavery? (For more information you might want to look at anti-slavery campaign websites such as <www.stopthetraffik.org>.)

Father, thank you for the freedom we enjoy. Forgive us when we have allowed others to be treated with less than the dignity for which you created them. Help us to see all people as your treasured possessions, and to work for an end to slavery and human trafficking in whatever form it may take. Amen.

Week five

Monday:	1 Cor. 1.1–17
Tuesday:	1 Cor. 1.18–31
Wednesday:	1 Cor. 2.1–9
Thursday:	Rom. 5.1–11
Friday:	Rom. 5.12–21
Saturday:	Rom. 6.1–14

Sunday reflection

The death of Jesus means much more than my own personal guarantee of heaven. It affects the whole of humanity, breaking down barriers that exist between Jew and non-Jew. More than that, it affects the whole cosmos, once enslaved to sin and corruption but now gloriously freed because of Jesus' death: a sacrifice that heals. This is the message with which we, like Paul, are entrusted and which we proclaim to the whole world. 'We represent the hope of the universe; which should make us sit up sharply.' Does it?

Lord Jesus, in this Lenten season we are reminded of the sacrifice you made for us. Thank you that, by your sacrifice, you have made peace between us and God, and between us and others. Help us to live as people who represent the hope of the universe. Amen.

Week six

Monday:	Rom. 8.1–11
Tuesday:	Rom. 8.12–30
Wednesday:	Rom. 8.31–39
Thursday:	Gal. 3.28—4.7
Friday:	Gal. 5.16–25
Saturday:	Gal. 6.1–10

Sunday reflection

'There is now no condemnation . . . the Spirit of life has set you free . . . we are children of God'! Romans chapter 8 is rightly one of the most-loved passages of Paul's letters. Here, Paul uses the language of 'first fruits' to describe the Christian life in the Spirit. To live according to the Spirit is therefore to live the life of the future new creation *in advance*. It is to be a people who live out 'heaven on earth'. Allow that truth to settle in your mind. How does that feel? And what might it look like?

Father, as we approach Holy Week we again thank you that, because of Jesus' sacrifice, there is now no condemnation for those who believe. Help us, as people delivered from condemnation, to live lives of faithful gratitude, not according to the flesh but according to the Spirit, knowing that nothing will be able to separate us from your love in Christ Jesus our Lord. Amen.

Week seven (Holy Week)

Monday:	Col. 1.1–20
Tuesday:	Col. 1.21–29
Wednesday:	Col. 2.1–15
Thursday:	2 Cor. 4.1–6
Good Friday:	2 Cor. 4.7–18
Holy Saturday:	2 Cor. 5.1–20

Resurrection Sunday reflection

In 1 Corinthians 15, a chapter you may want to read today, Paul writes perhaps his most powerful explanation of the importance of Jesus' resurrection. His point is this. The resurrection of Jesus matters, Paul says, because without it our faith is futile and we are pitiable people. The resurrection of Jesus matters because it is the first fruits of the resurrection of all people from the dead. The resurrection of Jesus matters because it guarantees the promise of a new creation. But not only that – it also inaugurates that new creation *now*, as a reality into which we are invited.

Lord Jesus, this Holy Week we have considered the depths of pain and despair that you experienced for us, and we are grateful. Help us to see in your sufferings the image of God, that we might know you better and more faithfully make you known.

On this Easter Sunday we announce your resurrection and your victory over evil and death. Let us live in this world as foretastes of the new creation to come, a world guaranteed by your resurrection life. Thanks be to God, who gives us the victory through our Lord Jesus Christ! Amen.

Notes

1 Probably the reason Paul's Jewish name is never given in Greek as 'Saulos' is that the word *saulos* could be used in some very disreputable senses.

2 See M. R. James, *The Apocryphal New Testament* (Oxford, Oxford University Press (revised), 1960), pp. 272–81 for the story of Paul and Thekla – a sort of historical novel about Paul; p. 273 for the description.

3 Tom Wright makes brilliant use of this little letter as a key to unlock the entire scheme of Paul's theology; see *Paul and the Faithfulness of God* (London, SPCK, 2013), Part I, Chapter 1.

4 See Tom Wright, *Paul and the Faithfulness of God*, Part IV, Chapter 15, especially pp. 1408–17 and 1443–9 for a very sophisticated and helpful discussion of this.

5 'And now, O Father, mindful of the love', by William Bright (no. 302 in *The English Hymnal*).

6 From 'Friday's Child', *Collected Poems* (London, Faber & Faber, 1994).

7 See *The Jewish Study Bible*, ed. Adele Berlin and Marc Zvi Brettler (Oxford, Oxford University Press, 2004), p. 415.

Suggestions for further reading

The literature on Paul is vast, and hugely diverse, but here are a few books that will give a good sense of the breadth and liveliness of the field.

N. T. Wright, *Paul and the Faithfulness of God* (London, SPCK, 2013).

Tom Wright's monumental, two-volume study covers all aspects of Paul's thinking with exceptional clarity and originality. Without doubt, it is one of the most important studies (ever?) of Paul's theological world, even if scholars continue to debate some of its arguments.

Robin Griffith Jones, *The Gospel According to Paul: The creative genius who brought Jesus to the world* (San Francisco, Harper SanFrancisco, 2004).

A lively and accessible study of Paul's life and thought that is especially good on the relation of Paul's theology to the mystical imagery of the Temple, the heavenly court and the restoration of God's image.

Among studies of individual letters of Paul:

Anthony C. Thiselton, *I Corinthians: A shorter exegetical and pastoral commentary* (Grand Rapids, Eerdmans, 2006).

A digest of the author's massive and authoritative commentary on the Greek text and a superb tool for understanding both Paul's theology and the society he writes in and for.

Ben Witherington III with Darlene Hyatt, *Paul's Letter to the Romans: A social–rhetorical commentary* (Grand Rapids, Eerdmans, 2004).
The authors provide finely detailed comment, with a solid theological interest.

A. Katherine Grieb, *The Story of Romans: A narrative defense of God's righteousness* (Louisville, KY, and London, Westminster John Knox Press, 2002).
Grieb locates Paul's arguments firmly against the background of the story of a God who keeps his promises.

And for general background:

Wayne A. Meeks, *The Moral World of the First Christians* (London, SPCK, 1987).
This study of how Christianity both assimilated and altered the moral assumptions of the classical world has stood the test of time very well and remains readable and valuable.